Praise for *Re-Engineering Your Life*:

An inspirational, uplifting, and empowering tribute to the power of taking control of your life. This book made me braver from the very first pages. The author inspires us to be more than we are, to take control of our lives, make better choices, and put aside our fears and negativity. The author's "can do" attitude is contagious, making us feel we can take control of our lives and make better choices. How much better our lives would be if we followed the author's advice!

—Wende A. Doniger, Ph.D., J.D.

re-engineering
your
life

nanette turner

re-engineering your life

to see and seize
opportunities

TATE PUBLISHING & *Enterprises*

This book is designed to provide accurate and authoritative information with regard to the subject matter covered. This information is given with the understanding that neither the author nor Tate Publishing, LLC is engaged in rendering legal, professional advice. Since the details of your situation are fact dependent, you should additionally seek the services of a competent professional.

The opinions expressed by the author are not necessarily those of Tate Publishing, LLC.

Published by Tate Publishing & Enterprises, LLC
127 E. Trade Center Terrace | Mustang, Oklahoma 73064 USA
1.888.361.9473 | www.tatepublishing.com

Tate Publishing is committed to excellence in the publishing industry. The company reflects the philosophy established by the founders, based on Psalm 68:11,
"The Lord gave the word and great was the company of those who published it."

Book design copyright © 2009 by Tate Publishing, LLC. All rights reserved.
Cover design by Lance Waldrop
Interior design by Jeff Fisher

Published in the United States of America

ISBN: 978-1-61566-428-3
1.Self-Help, Motivational & Inspirational
2. Self-Help, Personal Growth, General
09.11.23

Acknowledgments

It is with sincere gratitude that I extend my appreciation and thanks to:

My husband, Ira, for his unwavering support; my parents, Don and Halina Doiron, for their strength and opening my eyes to possibilities; and to my sisters, Michael and Renee, as their diverse and vibrant lives have been a joy to share.

My friends Debbie Henderson, Sheryl Wiereter, Barrie Sue Zicherman, and Laura McCozzi, each one a jewel of inspiration for me. I treasure our friendship.

Dr. Jean Clark and Dr. Barbara Morrell for their countless hours of insight and guidance.

And last but not least, without Abraham and Grace this book would not exist. Thank you for leading the way. I am looking forward to continuing our journey.

Table of Contents

Foreword

In a world of uncertainty and change, we as human beings often experience life's bruises. It is easy to feel overwhelmed and powerless. Nanette Turner reminds us to stay focused on what we want most and to create opportunities to fulfill them. She offers inspirational and poignant advice for personal growth and recovery. Life, as she reminds us, is often what we have made it, based on the choices that we have made. The opportunity and ability to re-engineer our lives is also in our control. So begin the pages and the process to go after the life you want.

—Barbara Morrell, Ph.D.

Introduction

In a time of economic crisis, millions of people around the world are finding themselves removed from the familiar; some having lost their jobs and homes. Many people are struggling, not sure which way to turn and have become desperate and despondent in the process. Yet human beings are resilient and creatively powerful. History has shown they can be very resourceful in rebuilding their lives, reshaping them in new and interesting ways. As this global world moves into a new phase, many aspects including the diversity offered by a borderless Internet, economic reform and the changing political climates worldwide have impacted our lives. These changes make it all the more important for you to look at where you are now in your life and consider how your viewpoint affects your abilities to not only to see, but also to seize the opportunities around you.

I am the navigator on the boat that my husband and I share. Having spent time navigating different waterways, my sailing experience has taught me that there are many ways to look at tackling issues, even if the hard facts do not change. By tweaking the sails and raising awareness to see the opportunities of wind and tide changes, all the while keeping a destination in mind, I have learned it is possible to get there even though it did not seem so at times. My husband has given me the nickname The Nagigator™. It was funny at first, but then I realized how appropriate it was. For any interest I had, by forcing myself to focus on it daily, I literally nagged at myself until little by little I was able to get things done. Figuring out how to get there and addressing the things that blocked my path and challenged my fears was indeed a journey, my own personal puzzle.

Each of us is unique, with our own history and circumstances. Each of us has a unique personal puzzle of complex experiences, desires, beliefs and emotions that affect us every day of our lives. All of us experience some level of anxiety and very few of us live a perfectly planned life. There are always detours and diversions popping up. Life takes us in different directions as circumstances present themselves, yet navigating our way through them can seem like an endless challenge of survival with little satisfaction in the journey. *By understanding the depth of awareness that you utilize in your day-to-day life, in the decisions you make and in the actions you take, you will be able to gain insights that will help you attain that which you want.* You can re-engineer yourself to achieve a more satisfying life, even in today's difficult circumstances. It is with this thought that I offer information and insights that many wish we had been told long ago. This book has been written in a short, powerful format to help you in the process of re-engineering your life. May each and every day of your life be an exciting and rewarding journey.

—The Nagigator™

Where Are You Now?

What is your everyday life like? Consider if it fulfilling, full of anticipation and if you wake up eager to meet the day, or if it is routine, ho-hum and maybe even dragging you down.

Do you ever ask yourself, *What happened? How did I get here at this point in my life?* Ever wake up thinking: *Wow, this isn't where I expected to be!* Often followed by: *Why didn't anyone tell me about (this or that)?* If you are not waking up each morning with a feeling of anticipation, eager and excited about the day and your future ahead, you are selling yourself short on one of the key joys of being human. It does not matter if your age is fifteen or fifty, if you are in school, college, just beginning a career, have been working for years and years, or even retired. Life isn't about waiting, life is about the *now!* Living your life in joy and anticipation, incorporating the things you want to do in your life *each and every day,* regardless of your daily routine or obligations, and looking forward to obtaining the lifestyle you envision *is within your ability!*

You may think that it isn't possible or that you are not in control, because big business, the economy, or others are in charge of your life. You may also think your day-to-day obligations take too much time to even consider the possibility of change. Perhaps it is time to reconsider. History has proven over and over again that people who are willing to step up and take an active part in shaping their own lives, can create opportunities out of all sorts of circumstances to achieve their dreams.

But just *how* do you do that? How many times have you tried to pursue your dream or goal only to get nowhere? You may have tried doing all the right things; gone to the right school, gotten the right job, married the right spouse, bought the right house, but you find you are still getting nowhere. How do you go after whatever it is you want when there are so many things that seem to block you? Money is always the big one, followed ever so closely by time. Then there is the economy, family and all the seemingly millions of things that get in the way. It makes you want to pop a pill, crawl back in bed and pull the covers over your head.

Life doesn't have to be that way! It can be exciting! It can be fun! Life is about living in joy! You are a human being with the innate ability to think and create. You are an individual with potential beyond even your current imagination. It's time for you to celebrate you. Yes, you! You are very important. Don't ever forget that. Your time here on this earth is very important and limited. Yes, you do have an expiration date, so are you going to make your time here fulfilling or ho-hum? Don't forget! Tomorrow is going to be very similar to today, this year to last year, *unless you do something.* Now is the time to do something about it. So where do you start?

Start with you. There is no magic wand that can zap it all together for you. You are unique and being so means that you need to understand your very unique personal puzzle, the stuff that makes you the one and only *you*. Your sense of well-being and satisfaction with your life comes from a number of areas including family, friends, work, hobbies, health, prosperity, social status, desires and so forth. Each of these *contributes to* and is *influenced by* your experiences and choices. Every single one of these has its own challenges. Understanding how these things affect you and re-engineering them to better suit your dreams is key to achieving what you want. *Most of us just don't get that, which is why so very few of us excel.* Some people achieve their dreams against incredible odds, but most just settle for something less. Most people live boring, predictable lives, often living vicariously through the lives of others or through books, newspapers, TV or movies. They will sit week after week, hooked on a TV show as entertainment, while their lifetime passes them by. They have numerous excuses and justifications for not doing anything else. They become frustrated that their lives are not as interesting or exciting as what they view on the TV, and their frustration then gets enacted out by creating drama in their lives that becomes counter productive and detrimental to themselves and others.

Your life is too precious to not be living it to your fullest potential, to be excited about it. Yet you can be manipulated by influences in your life. The scary part is many of those influences you may not be aware of or have never really given thought to, but they can sidetrack you from achieving that which you really are interested in doing. *You need to take a hard look at where you are right now, because where you are right now, right this minute is a result of those experiences and choices you have made in the past.* If you want to change your present life situation, you have to comprehend the influences in your life and learn how to modify your choices and your actions in order to get what you want.

Change does not mean that you have to become a different person. You are a treasure just as you are. To excel in your life, to achieve the things you want to do, you can re-engineer aspects of your life, tweaking them gradually with subtle modifications that help you move closer to your goals. Change does not happen without effort, but re-engineering is not a difficult process. It does require that you become aware of your thoughts, actions and how you spend your time, all the while making small changes to build a stronger foundation from which you can move forward with conviction and determination to achieve what you want. The re-engineering steps in the following chapters will provide you insights into your life as it is now and see where you can choose to make changes which may broaden your perspective to seize new opportunities.

Real satisfaction in your life does not come without effort. No one can hand it to you. No one can do it for you. Many of the rich and famous will attest to that. So to get from point A to wherever it is that you want to be, you need to start with you. Find the keys to open those doors on your way to achieving your fulfilling life. Learn to understand your personal puzzle. You might be very surprised to find out what is actually keeping you from your desires.

It's time for you to get on track, get excited and go after the life you want!

Do you really know?

Very few people ever take a moment in their life to seriously contemplate what exactly it is they are interested in, what they want in life, much less define it and spend time focusing on it. Many have a vague idea, a dream or a wish, but most are caught up in the day to day activities and are struggling to keep a roof over their head, food on the table and keep up with all their obligations. Yet, by not taking some time out and investing in yourself, you exist with vague and most often an unfulfilled version of the life you would really like to be living.

What does the vision of your ideal life look like? Do you really know? And just where are you now in your vision? What does your roadmap to achieving that vision look like, or do you even have one? Surprisingly, most of us do not.

You may move in a general direction, occasionally pushed by circumstances seemingly beyond your control, never reaching your potential. It's like a boat adrift on the seas without a rudder, forced to drift whichever way the wind and current takes it. You may feel you are without power, without choices, subject to demands from other people and your current circumstances.

But what if you were able to take back a little control? What if you dipped your toe in the water and found a way to bring focus back into your life, by learning how to correct your sails to navigate where you want to be? *What if it is possible to change your course, by choice, to whatever degree you want?*

A change in course does not have to be monumental. It can be as small as having the ability to do one small thing daily that brings you joy, or it can be as large as you envision. Neither can come about unless you put some thought into it.

Begin The Process of Re-Engineering

So what are your interests? What are those things that bring a spark of joy and excitement when you think about the possibility of incorporating them into your life? Think about what makes your pulse race and your mind light up with ideas! Our thoughts move like the wind, and ideas can be fleeting. Capture those thoughts, those ideas. The process of re-engineering begins by putting them down on paper so you can work with them and see where they lead you. Think of them with no regard for your own personal challenges; physical, mental, environmental, skill level or monetary. None of that matters. *What matters is that you take the time to define your personal vision of your life.* By writing it down, you're laying the basic groundwork. You are able to focus on your ideas, expand upon them, and continue molding them into a reality you can create. Regardless of how big or how foolish you think your ideas are, write them down, don't hold back.

Start Your List

Call it *Interests.* For this list, focus on what you want to be *doing.* Underneath it all, what are you really interested in doing with your time? Consider what is going to give you that sense of accomplishment and satisfaction. What is the key piece that excites you, makes you happy, and motivates you when you think about it? List out all of the things you can. Let your mind wander. Don't let any practical thoughts limit your list. If it is something you would like to do, put it down on the list. Nothing is out of reach.

Keep the list with you as you go through your day, adding to it as thoughts come up. Like most people, you may have difficulty starting this process or clarifying exactly what you want. That's okay. Continue to work with the list over time and let your imagination help you expand on it. Constantly assess things around you, check your interest level for any thought your mind continually goes back to.

Creating a vague list will only get you a vague life path, one that is easily sidetracked and usually unfulfilling. Wishing to be an artist will not make you one. Detail out exactly what you want. If it is an artist, think of what kind, where, and what aspects can help you get there. List out any schools or training that you may need. Consider any connections you have. There are many different ways to achieve a goal, be creative. The purpose of making the list is to create your life through your ideas, wants and desires. The list will help you clarify your ideas, allowing you to fully define and expand upon them. They are your creation, no one else's. As a human being, you will constantly be creating, thinking, growing and changing. In order to achieve any of your dreams, you need to really focus. Think about the things that excite you and that you are passionate about! Don't let it be a passing thought. *Focus on it, write it out, expand on it!*

Remember that all humans have the innate ability to create. One thought will often lead to another, then another. Our minds are constantly working. Have you ever experienced a time when your mind is working on a thought completely unrelated to what you are doing? Time passes and you realize you were so lost in the thought, you can't remember what you were just doing. Your creative ability stems from deep within the core of your being. Your thoughts are unique. Let the ideas flow. Contemplate any one item on your list and consider the variations. One thought, one idea could grow to a variety of different aspects. Any subject has dozens of options. If you only have one item on your list, you are really selling yourself short. Avoid tunnel vision and be open in your thoughts. Do some research; check the magazines, the advertisements, the stores. Talk with people. Look at everything around you. A seed of an idea will expand and grow in various directions from a core idea. It can almost achieve a life of its own, with threads of opportunity reaching out in all directions. Keep digging and be as detailed as you can.

Once your *Interests* list is filled out, it is time to prioritize it. First, spend some time reviewing the list and brainstorming options and opportunities to each of the items you have listed. Make sure you have listed all the aspects that interest you. Once that is complete, go through the list and consider which item is the most important to you. It does not have to be practical; it just has to resonate deep inside you as what would be the most satisfying thing to do. If you keep this item in focus through the remainder of this book, you will begin to recognize the influences in your life that have colored your choices and actions, keeping you from your goal. You will then be able to see where you can apply the re-engineering process to make progress toward achieving what it is you want to do. Now that you have your list, and the item that is the most important to you forefront in your mind, the next step in the process is raising your level of awareness so that you can understand and see that you do have other choices and opportunities.

Your Level of Awareness

Awareness has been defined as a consciousness, a knowing. When you think of awareness, you may consider yourself understanding of the basics of right and wrong. You also know when you are hot or cold, hungry or tired, happy, impatient, angry or frustrated. You are aware on the surface level of what you are doing.

You probably consider yourself to be a person who is aware of all that is going on around you and in the decisions you make, but more often than not, you probably move through life on auto-pilot. You take an action, doing or saying something without consciously connecting that action to a deeper meaning or what the consequences are.

For instance: When you use a credit card to purchase an item, you obtain the item thinking of what you intend to use it for. Your thoughts are focused on what you will be doing with the item.

When you eat dinner, your thoughts are focused on the food and the company, enjoying the tastes, the smells, the conversation and the atmosphere.

When you have a drink, you enjoy the relaxing effect of the alcohol, maybe even feel a little more likely to express yourself.

As a human, your mind pushes your thoughts aside so that you can enjoy the moment. You selectively do this over and over and over again on autopilot, creating a habitual process you are comfortable with. Without thinking about the consequences, you compound your problems. You say to yourself, *Just this once* or *One more time* or *Next week, next month I'll do it differently.* When the bill arrives, to you, it is a *totally separate action taking place!* A completely different day and time from when the credit card was used. Mail becomes the culprit, bringing a bill to pay for an item that was purchased long ago and has probably been long forgotten. In the morning, it is the scale you step on that displays those nasty numbers or it is the clothing you try to get into that has become much too tight, or it is the mirror reflecting a view of yourself that does not please you. Then there is the effect of the alcohol, which can be either long term with damage to your liver, or have a more immediate affect when you realize the next day you have totaled your car. The mail, the scale, the clothing, the mirror, your health or the car have become your default focus, where you choose to lay the blame. These are events that seem to be new and separate experiences, but are actually consequences of your prior actions.

This mental veil is not living in the state of awareness. *It is putting your mind in a soft haze that somehow makes you think that you are relieved of responsibility for the choices you make and the actions you take, which are contrary to your true desires.* These examples are typical of so many things you do in your life on autopilot. With your awareness and your focus dimmed, you are often living in a reactive state, not consciously aware of your actions and therefore not feeling responsible for them. In the back of your mind, you think it's something that just happened. It is no wonder that so many people are in debt, overweight, or have addictions like alcoholism. The depressed "I don't care" autopilot kicks in with irrational thoughts and excuses. You may consider yourself a victim of society and feel limited in your choices. You might not take action when options present themselves that could change your life. This type of autopilot living *is allowing your past influences to make your present choices!*

Re-Engineering Your Level of Awareness

Each day is a new beginning, a new chance for change to achieve your dreams. You must be aware of what you are doing every day, throughout the day and comprehend the results of the choices you are making *as you make them* in order to truly make changes in your life. Get off of autopilot. Wherever you are in your life right now, like it or not, you have settled into a routine.

To help get off of autopilot and out of your

routine, shake it up. Look at your daily routine. Take a look at it with an awareness of how everything can or will be affected by what you are interested in doing. Some people feel they do not have the luxury of time to make any effort. The first step of just becoming aware of what your choices and actions are in your daily routine will not affect your time. To begin with, it is only a matter of seconds here and there as thoughts flow through your mind, which will not impact upon your day. Start by just being aware.

Consider your daily routine. You get up at a certain time, go through your morning listening to the same news, reading the same paper, eating the same breakfast. You go off to where you spend your day, never really noticing how you traveled to and arrived there from your home. You are comfortable in your routine. Yet that simple routine from the time your eyes opened in the morning to the time you arrived at the place you go to every day, which may have taken minutes to let's say an hour or so, was full of opportunities. Did you notice them? Did you notice there was a segment on TV or the radio that directly related to what is on your *Interests* list as you prepared to leave your home in the morning? Perhaps not, since you did not check to see what was available. Instead, you listened to the same old station.

Did you notice the places on the way of your morning journey; the streets, the homes, the businesses? What about the people? Friends, relatives, neighbors—even strangers. The store clerk, the driver; they have all had experiences, influences and made choices. Don't let social or economic barriers exist. Talk with them and share your interests. Remember the degrees of separation. The person you pass by may be the catalyst for your next step to achieving something on your list, or maybe they know someone who is. You may be only a contact or two away from someone who could have an impact on your vision. When you serve someone, assist them, or help them, you build a network of people interested in helping you. You build character. Word is passed on about you, your interests and your plans. Connections are made.

You can make subtle changes each day that move you closer to your desires that will not impact on your time and in doing so, provide you with a sense of anticipation and eagerness, which spark further creativity in your thoughts. Don't become so blinded by routine, that you cannot see how you are holding yourself back. So make the changes in your daily routine. They need not be dramatic. Just be aware. Then as you focus on being aware, being in the present moment, you will begin to notice things, and make connections to ideas and possibilities to achieve the things you are interested in. By being more engaged in life, sharing, growing and learning about the things that are of interest to you, your enthusiasm will grow. Soak in the world around you. Be in the present moment. Being aware is being alive! Make choices while you are in the state of awareness. Know why you are making them. *Understand that choices occur not only at the major crossing points in your life. Choices are made every day, every hour, every minute! Most of the time you are not even aware you are making them!*

Re-Engineer Your Thoughts

Pay attention to what you do and why you do it. It enables you to evaluate your choices and actions. Can you make a different decision, have a different perspective or reaction that would alter the outcome of whatever it is you are doing? Surprisingly, yes.

For example, if someone says something to you that bothers you, you have choices. You can ignore it or you can address it. Always look to yourself first. Have your past actions or words invited such comments, or have you allowed someone to treat you the way they do? Once you have looked at the situation from all angles, you can then consider what changes, if any, you would like to make. In doing so, you can also consider how you would address the situation. Snapping back in anger or hurt only aggravates the situation. Reacting quickly may not produce desirable consequences. Allowing it to continue may cause further distress. Speaking with quiet respect, dignity and in a warm friendly manner may be a better choice. Then again, sometimes it is truly not important enough to give further thought to and you can just walk away. The choices are yours.

Living your life in full awareness allows you to focus on what is best for you. It allows you to make decisions and focus on what is important to you, giving you some control over the outcome of any given moment. Many people actually do not apply this, living by default, reacting to situations, rather than stepping back and taking a proactive choice to that with which they are faced. If you find that you are constantly reacting to situations in a tense, volatile roller coaster state, you are letting situations and your emotions control you. You are subject to being manipulated by other influences. This can be as simple as a comment someone said to a traumatic event that happened. Be aware that you can choose your thoughts and actions. You can control your emotions and you can influence others.

Here is a very simple process. When you wake up in the morning, just lay in bed for a few minutes. Think about the day. What is the weather going to be like? Beautiful? Good; appreciate it. Maybe snowy or icy? Feelings of negativity may creep in. Focus on the good side; maybe the snow looks beautiful, you have warm clothes, it's part of a season that rejuvenates the earth. Whatever works for you. In other words, *pull the positive from the negative.* How you feel at any given time *affects your decision process.* As your thoughts continue, you think about the day ahead. Maybe someone related to the day pops in your mind who you do not like or want to deal with. Try a different perspective. Have you ever tried to find out about them, or their interests? Maybe today would be a good day to try and improve that relationship. You never know what it might lead to, perhaps a connection to something or someone in line with your dreams. Every thought has options and every situation has opportunities.

The point here is that even when it seems difficult, be aware of your negative thoughts and find a way to flip them to a positive one. Look at whatever it is that is undesirable around you, any problem or situation, *as an opportunity.* Create a solution. Create five different solutions. You have that ability. There is never only one choice. Take the time to contemplate what you may be facing in the day and be proactive.

You can let negative thoughts and emotions rule and ruin your day, or you can choose something better. No matter how tough, unpleasant, or bad the situation is, you can always focus on something that will improve your experience and quite possibly open you up to new opportunities. First, you must be aware of your thoughts and actively be in control of them, while you seek out solutions from a positive perspective. This can be difficult for many. For example, you may have financial worries on your mind, then slipped and fell in the rain on your way to work, tearing your suit. To top it off, you have missed the bus. On and on, your thoughts can spiral down, causing feelings of anger and despair. Stop it! Take a deep breath and make the decision to change your perspective. Take a look around and appreciate what you have, maybe there are some finance options you have yet to investigate, maybe you did not like the suit to begin with and the rain is saving you money by watering the lawn. On the next bus, you may meet someone who knows someone that can help you with whatever it is you are interested in. Put a smile on your face, even if it is derived from the ironic humor of your situation. Keep your item from your *Interests* list in your head and the excitement of anticipation of doing it in your heart. Concentrate on viewing situations as opportunities and engage people around you in your life.

The Re-Engineering Art
of Spiraling Upward

Being aware of your feelings and controlling your thoughts to alter your feelings to a more positive state is a very powerful tool. By taking small steps in your thought process, finding those positive thoughts, and expand on them by deliberately choosing and focusing on them, you can re-engineer your mind. Do not dwell on the negative! Do not engage in conversation about it over and over again! If that is all you can think about and talk about, that is all you will ever see and receive. It is a waste of your time and others'. When you feel bad and find your mind leading you into a continuing down-ward spiral of negativity, worry or anger, *stop it!* Force your thoughts away. Look to your feelings and move away from what makes you feel bad. Move toward whatever it is that makes you feel good, no matter how trivial or stupid you think it is. It may only be remembering the antics of a puppy, a great play in a game or appreciating the lines of a sports car. Continue those thoughts, find more and more to appreciate. Remembering a funny movie or good times with friends. Make yourself laugh and hold onto that feeling. Focus on positive thoughts. Build on them to pull yourself out of the negative. Create an upward spiral of good thoughts in your mind. By being aware of your thoughts and deliberately choosing a positive path, you will gain a new viewpoint and will then be able to see opportunities. Your attitude and behavior will attract the interest of others, providing you with even more options.

Being Aware of Choices

Now, as you go through your routine, you are aware it is a routine that you can alter. Each day you may try something different. Move from being a zombie to being interactive and interested in what is going on around you. But even more importantly, do it with awareness. As you move through your life interacting with others, be aware of the thoughts, feelings, actions and choices you are making. These are key to re-engineering your life. Each is a step toward a better path. Keep the priority item from your *Interests* lists foremost in your mind. When you make choices in your day based on the inspiration you feel about your priority interest, the excitement and anticipation of moving toward your interest takes hold and fear takes a back seat.

Again, be aware that your past influences directly affect your present choices, which is why the following chapters are critical. They bring to light the influences that surround you and can unknowingly sway your choices. If you are not aware of them, then you are not consciously making the best choices to achieve the life you dream about and to do the things you desire.

Family Influences

The family environment, the people you grew up with, and the atmosphere of those experiences had a tremendous impact on you. Some of it is very obvious, but even more interesting are the not-so-obvious attitudes and behaviors that you have learned or adopted into your life that color your world, some good, others creating barriers to obtaining that which you want. They drive your thought process, your choices, and they affect you *every single day of your entire life.* Most of the time you are not even aware of it. It is important that you are consciously aware of these influences and take action to accept or change where change is needed. You must think about it, be aware. Don't criticize it, just know what those influences are and make sure your future choices are influenced by what *you* choose to focus on, not some old thought in the back of your head that does not serve your purpose.

Unconditional Love and Expectations

No matter how you have chosen to live your life, a family typically offers unconditional love. Whether you do well or not by your own judgement or theirs, they will continue to influence your life. They may offer advice and support, or they may yell and scream if your choices are not the same as theirs. Regardless, the words spoken will have an impact on you and as the years pass, you may find yourself not living up to your own expectations, much less that of your family. This measuring up can feel like a heavy burden. In order to release it, you need to make a shift in your thinking. Whenever you have expectations, whether it is how a family gathering should go, or an achievement of some sort, you set yourself up for the possibility of disappointment. Expectations look for pre-determined results. You have no more control over others than they do of you, so expecting someone to behave in a certain manner will often lead to disappointment. What you are in control of is your own thoughts. Make the shift in thinking from expectation to appreciation. By appreciating others for who they are and where they are in their life right now, you open up to acceptance, which encourages growth and dialogue. More importantly, having the ability to appreciate yourself, where you are in your life right now, opens your mind to see opportunities for your future.

The shift to appreciation of yourself can be difficult. Years of thoughts, both good and bad may be programmed in your mind. Uncover what those thoughts are by being aware of what you are thinking and feeling at all times. Root them out. You may have been told that you are pretty or ugly. Guess what; people who have been told both have succeeded in obtaining their dream. The same is true for stupid and smart. Look at how many successful people never had a formal education. Look at how many unsuccessful people with formal degrees are miserable in their lives. Be aware of those automatic *I can't* statements that run in your head. Once you identify the unwanted statements and recognize their negative influence, you can throw them out and replace them with a positive one. Easier said than done? Not really. As long as you understand that you have control over your mind, then you will be able to do it. When the negative thought or worry comes to mind and you are in a state of awareness of your thoughts, you can choose to change them by offering your mind thoughts of appreciation of who you are and what you have right now, and the anticipation of seeking out new opportunities. Use the spiral up technique to shift to positive thoughts. You and only you, have the ability to control your thoughts.

So find out what the influences are from your family. Why do you have the beliefs that you do? Are they adopted from someone else or did you make a conscious decision based on a factual analysis of the data available and then determine from that what *you* believe? Many live in societies where they must conform to certain standards for the sake of their existence. While you may be in such a situation and for a time have to conform, you are still in control of your mind and can use the time by continuing to gather information and create options to prepare for your future. Research can be done while still respecting the family environment in which you live.

The family unit itself can contain members with beliefs that vary widely. Understand that you do not have to voice your beliefs; it is enough that you believe the way you do. It is not your journey to impress your will upon others, nor is it theirs. Parents have a parental obligation in raising their children to impart knowledge to help the child. As an adult, you can learn to live in harmony and accept that someone can believe differently. Embrace diversity and use it to your advantage!

The family unit is a training ground for your interaction with society as a whole. What you learn in the family unit may or may not serve you well in society. No one gets to choose their family. What is important is how you choose to deal with it and how you let it influence you. For some, families are people you probably would not have chosen. Yet, you can learn to love and appreciate the diversity over time. That diversity exposes you to thoughts and beliefs of which you would otherwise have no firsthand knowledge. But there are critical elements that come into play. One is an auto-response behavior to any given situation. Children learn from parental influence how to deal with situations, usually adopting a negative behavior without question. This can be anything from offering a silent response or negative teasing, to unwarranted volatile reactions of yelling and even to the extreme of physical abuse. As they grow into young adults, many are capable of re-evaluating the behavior, controlling themselves, and making the choice to behave in a better manner. Others have never given thought to the automatic response that can be triggered at any time. They feel the behavior is acceptable and continue with it, simply because that is how they learned it. Or it has become a habit, developed over time, even though the behavior or habit no longer serves a purpose. The process of learning should never stop. *Being aware of your behavior allows you to modify your actions and reactions in order to achieve the results you want.* In order to achieve your goals, be aware of your behavior and see where you can re-engineer changes that will put you on a proactive path rather than a reactive one.

The Influence of Memories

Another area of family influence or events from your childhood that may be affecting your current day-to-day life is past memories. Some adults, on thinking of their childhood, have unhappy memories that immediately come to the surface, which may easily be interpreted as a bad childhood. Others have a good or average childhood, having had a home, food, clothing, toys and probably quite a bit of laughter provided for by their parents. Memories are built on the natural instinct of protection and survival. What this means is that those childhood experiences that are painful are utmost in our minds, *because they taught us something.* They allow our protective instincts to kick in to remind us to be wary. Being yelled at or having behavior corrected in some manner sets a memory. A lesson was being learned and the basic human survival instinct registers it as a caution in our mind, always bringing it to the front of our memories. Now as an adult, you need to be in control. You need to put these memories in the proper perspective. Acknowledge that a lesson was learned or that a bad event happened and close the door on it. Recognize it for what it is, a bad memory, and choose to stop it. Look closer at your childhood to find happier memories. Select a few that may bring a smile to your face. Have them ready to use in replacement when the bad memories pop in. When the bad memory arrives, do not dwell on it. Dismiss it and replace it with the good.

If you have been abused, it is harder to gain control. The bad memories are stronger. But you have a choice. A choice of either letting the memory control you, or you gaining control over it and your life. There are phenomenal stories of people who have overcome terrible experiences, having chosen to focus on the future instead of the past. For many of these people it has taken a great deal of inner strength each and every day to move forward. This is a conscious choice they have made, facing it each and every time it comes up by refusing to dwell on it or allowing it to take any more of their present life by speaking of it. Instead, they have rebuilt and strengthened their inner thought process, choosing to look forward and focus on the future and what they are interested in.

Your Future Starts Now

The choices you make going forward will determine your future. Good and bad events color your choices. The things you do or do not do are based on them. Choose what you think about. Choose to drop habits that no longer serve you now. Close the door on thoughts that do not serve a purpose to you now. When you find yourself reliving a bad memory in your mind and feeling yourself sucked into a bad place, internally shout the word *Stop!* Refuse to let those thoughts take hold and banish them from your mind *each and every time they come up.* Appreciate the past, but live in the present and look toward the future. No one is obligated to do anything for you. This is your life, your choices. Take control and concentrate on thoughts that serve you now. Refuse to let the past take up precious time in your current daily life. Refuse to let bad events change the color of your day. Replace them with your dreams of what you choose to do. Think of the future and focus on the one item you selected as your priority from your *Interests* list. Detail it out in your mind, and consider all the steps you can think of to make it happen. Feel the energy as your mind fills with anticipation and creative thought. Focus on the feeling of excitement, the spark of anticipation. You can choose to do this as often as needed.

For some, it may be hard to appreciate and treasure the experiences with your family unit. Understand that you have gained insight to how others think and act that you would never have been exposed to if it had not been for them. Their thoughts and choices may or may not be similar to yours, but the experience of being around others over a period of time is an insightful education that can serve you in future situations.

It is important to understand that you are *not* who your family is, you are *not* what your job is, you are *not* what your financial status is, and you are not whatever it is that has happened to you in the past. You *are* what *you choose to do.* And successfully doing something that interests you without harming anyone else in the process is where you will feel a sense of satisfaction. Once you can understand this and put your family unit in perspective, you will be more aware of its influence over you and you will be better equipped to deal with it.

Know that you cannot change your past family experiences any more that you can change your family members. By putting your family life in a clear perspective, you can re-engineer your thoughts and actions. You can learn to dismiss and ignore any statements that push your auto response buttons by deciding not to wallow in and address past transgressions. You can choose to look toward the future and work on establishing stronger relationships using the tools in the following chapters.

Relationships Matter

Your relationships with other people are a major factor in defining your character. Those relationships can also have a positive or negative affect on your life and the achievement of your interests. Whom you choose to be around and share your life with is a very important choice. There is a chapter further on about your social network, but this chapter will concentrate on the one-on-one relationship with your life partner, the person with whom you seek to share your life's experiences.

That one-on-one relationship can be very elusive to obtain and once entered into, even harder to hold on to. Millions of dollars have been made in the relationship industry, but there are several things you should be aware of that are typically ignored which are vital to your success in this area.

Let's start with character. Human character is complex and it can be illustrated in the tangible evidence of beliefs and values that are demonstrated in our daily lives through our speech and actions. Everyone has it. Some are good, strong and earn respect of others. Then there are other types of character that are not so attractive.

Understanding your own character by observing yourself among others can be an enlightening experience. You need to be aware of what your own actions reveal about yourself. How you act and react to situations is what defines your character. Your tone of voice, expressions, body language, choice of words and actions are an expression of your beliefs and thoughts, drawing results to you, which can then influence you either negatively or positively and take control over your life. If you want to enter into or improve a relationship, you must first understand that you cannot change anyone else. The only person you can change is you. However, your actions and reactions can influence your partner as well. Have a good understanding of your own character before you work on building a successful relationship with another by spending some time in self-observation. A little re-engineering in some simple steps can go a long way to creating and maintaining a happier relationship.

An Exercise in the Visual and Audio Components of Character

Take some time over the next few weeks and see how your character appears to others.

Tone of Voice: Determine if your voice conveys interest, is enthusiastic and caring, or if it is monotone, bored, irritated or even angry.

Facial Expressions: Consider how often you smile and laugh. Check for negative habits like scowling or rolling of your eyes. Often times they are done out of habit, yet can have a negative influence on others.

Body Language: Be aware of your body language when you are around others. Notice if you maintain eye contact or do you look away as if in boredom. Think about how you greet others and consider if you smile, shake hands, hug and pay attention to the other person. Be aware of who is around you, if you are turning your back on someone.

Choice of Words: See how often you use "I" or "You" statements. When relating to someone, tackling a problem from an "I" perspective: *I feel, I think, I need,* is always more palatable to the other person than "You" statements; *You need, you should.* Determine if you are initiating conversations in public that should be private so as not to embarrass the person to whom you are speaking with. Waiting to speak to someone can help you control your emotions and consider both sides before addressing an issue. Also rein in on the foul language. When spoken, it may seem like an apt expression of your thoughts, yet to the receiver, you may appear hostile, crude and uneducated, which are not traits upon which to build a relationship.

Actions and Reactions: Check out your behavior to see if your actions are considerate and respectful of others. See if you listen to others and try to understand their perspective or if you are too busy trying to get your own point across that you constantly interrupt them. True respect is always earned based on how you treat others. Be aware of your reactions, especially to negative situations. See if anger, tantrums and violence come quickly, or if you take the time to think before you act, giving consideration to others and showing that consideration in your reaction and choice of words.

In the process of re-engineering your life, this assessment of your character and a willingness to maintain an awareness of these five audio and visual components that you have complete control over can become your greatest asset. Not only will it help you in the one-on-one relationship, but in all aspects of your life, as you can positively influence others which will help open doors to opportunities.

The Tells

When you enter into a relationship with your life partner, you need to pay attention. Often, the initial impression you receive when you are around someone is favorable, simply because you project the image in your mind of how you want to see the person, ignoring or dismissing contradictory evidence. There are always clues to the core character of a person and understanding that character is a key to the relationship. For example, someone you spend time with may always be charming to you, yet sharp, crude or arrogant to others. You may experience this view when you are at a restaurant or some social event. It is only when you spend some time with someone, paying attention to their actions and interactions with others that you are able to ascertain their character. Regardless of how they interact with you in the beginning, over the long haul, how they interact with others will eventually be how they interact with you. So pay attention to all the details.

It's important to note here that it is about actions and words. Actions are the *tells*. You probably have heard of tells in the poker world of gaming. They are the small signs a player unknowingly gives off about the status of his or her cards, which informs the observer what the player may or may not be thinking about the cards they are holding. In poker, it may be the nervous twitch on the face or the biting of the lip. It takes a keen eye of observation to pick up on some of these tells. In relationships, tells can show us by action if they really do support the words spoken. Words can support the actions or belie them. Words on the other hand, weave their way into our minds. Words can create harmony, peace and trust, or they can destroy them. Both actions and words will have an influence on you. It is your choice how you handle that influence.

Consideration

Once you have moved beyond the character assessment of the person in whom you are interested, you need to understand that you are moving from a singular focus of only your needs, to one that must consider the views of the other individual. A successful relationship is one where the two parties involved are *aware*. They are aware of their own views and that of their partner. They do not have to agree with the other person's viewpoint, but they are aware that they have choices and they care enough to negotiate a compromise. They are also aware that each is a unique individual with interests of their own, and the freedom to enjoy those interests as long as they are not detrimental to their partner. It is critical to the success of the relationship that both views are considered. This means that you are *considerate* of the other person. They must mean something to you; you must care about their perspective, otherwise what is the point of the relationship?

Being considerate shows in your willingness to truly listen to the other person, to be patient, to consider their viewpoint and to really care about it. It shows in your choice of words, in your tone of voice, *even under pressure*. It shows in how you speak about the person, whether you keep your issues to yourself or speak highly or negatively of your partner to others.

Those who live with inconsiderate partners have difficulty in finding balance in their lives. It is always about a test of wills, a battle of who is more dominant. One may always have the need to prove who is right or wrong. Ego gets involved and consideration goes out the door. At any given time one or the other is dissatisfied. Proving right or wrong or rubbing someone's nose in an issue is not caring or considerate, and even if you think you are right, by forcing the issue, you loose in the long run. There is always more than one way of doing something. If the ego is not involved, some partners may just be apathetic. They may pretend to care, but refuse to compromise or even negotiate. Relationships require consideration to balance the needs of each individual. Relationships and the individuals involved in them need constant attention to grow. Those with falsely busy lives tend to fall into the trap of not making the time to invest in the relationship. Schedules become so busy; consideration for the relationship and their partner is not first and foremost in their every day life. Guard against this. Make it a point to spend time with your partner every single day.

Relationships will begin to wane when one individual gives up their interests for the sake of another. Great amounts of talent have been lost by this type of stifling. Over time, relationships can also deteriorate by falling into a routine. When a relationship becomes comfortable, eventually one partner will feel unappreciated, especially when little focus is paid to their needs. Resentment builds and the relationship suffers, often as a surprise to the other partner. If you are feeling resentment, you need to go look in the mirror. You always have choices. If your voice is not being heard in the relationship, you have choices of how to deal with it. Find out why you are not being heard. Are you not expressing your interests, speaking up for what you want, or are your actions in doing so not considerate of the other individual? When you approach someone in a hostile or angry manner, typically they will shut down, effectively closing communication. When treated this way, why would anyone want to do anything for you? Also, if your behavior is unpredictable, communication will cease as your partner is walking on eggshells and would not be comfortable opening up. Only after you have pointed the finger at yourself and seriously evaluated your actions and words, then and only then should you look to your partner to find fault. Even then, know that you cannot change anyone else but yourself. If you determine that your partner is at fault, the only thing you can do is change your own thoughts, your attitude, and your behavior. Change *your* approach to the subject with *your* tone, attitude, and words. Careful consideration on your part can help you achieve the results you want.

Respect and Testing

In order to have a successful relationship, you need to work together with *respect* for each other. That respect is born out of appreciation for each other's character and the consideration given to each other at all times. Respect is earned. It is earned over time with actions and words. Respect is shown through acceptance of each other's individuality, encouraged through a nurturing, safe environment that is free from ridicule, teasing and oppression. It shows in the appreciation spoken to each other, and is demonstrated in the acceptance of who the person is and their interests. Respect grows and becomes trust. That trust grows over the years, drawing two people incredibly closer. Trust builds and deepens the relationship, allowing it to grow even more, giving the two parties more confidence and freedom to open up further, experience more together and grow ever closer to each other. This is often seen in couples, who after time, cannot bear to be apart. The relationship has built to such an incredible value, that it has become the single most important and satisfactory component of their lives. Everything else revolves around it through consideration, respect and a balancing act of interests.

Early on in a relationship, adults are all like children. They test the boundaries. What can you get away with? It is critical to be aware of this aspect of human nature. Be aware of your actions. Somewhere in the course of constructing the relationship, a boundary of trust and respect will be tested. It is important to acknowledge it, set the standard and live by it. If you let it pass, when your partner disrespects you, or if you make a habit of doing this to them, the foundation of your relationship is flawed and it will never achieve its full potential. However, once addressed, put it behind you. Nothing is gained by throwing old issues in someone's face over and over. It is not positive, nor is it forward-looking. Step away from the negative past and choose to reach for a positive future. Respect *and the trust gained from it* are fragile. Both can be destroyed instantly, damaged beyond repair.

There is an old analogy of giving a thirsty man a cup of water. Cool and refreshing. Yet the bearer puts one tiny drop of something bad in the water. Just a tiny drop, but the drink is destroyed.

No matter how good it could have been, that one action destroyed it. This type of action happens constantly in relationships, undermining the foundation. All the generous words and actions that you give in a relationship can be similarly wiped out by one tiny word or action of disrespect. Referring to your partner with a derogatory name or a statement of "You're wonderful, but ..." is the type of thing that breaks apart the foundation of the relationship.

One negatively spoken word is clearly heard and engrained in our mind, *even though thousands of positive words were spoken before and after it!* Be aware and guard against taking this route. You will be surprised how hard it is. Every human is sensitive to this, no matter how hard or strong they appear. A negative word or statement can tear apart a relationship in the blink of an eye. This is where the difficulty of relationships lay. Not in your heart, but in your words and actions, every day, for as long as you both shall live. Choose your words and timing as carefully as you would want someone to choose for you. Focus on the positive. When you have to address a negative, flip it to focus on the positive, as to what you would like or appreciate. Be careful in your tone and body language. Speak to others as you would like to be spoken to.

Expectations and Acceptance

Be careful of having false expectations of your partner to fulfill some vague idea of something you want from them, or how you want them to behave. People involved in a relationship typically go into it with expectations. They have in their mind how their partner will behave, including how the should dress and act in social situations. They also have in mind how their partner should handle any given situation, such as paying bills or dealing with an irate person. What each person expects from a relationship can be vastly different. Having discussions and learning what is comfortable for each other and being accepting of differences is key. Learn the art of balancing your strengths and weaknesses as you define your roles, keeping in mind to ignore trivial things and accept and appreciate the important things. Often one partner will make an effort to take care of an issue, even though it is not their strong skill. They may mess it up terribly. Keep in mind that things probably can be fixed and *they are only things*. What is important to the relationship is that the effort was made. Appreciate that and show them your appreciation! Avoid pointing out shortcomings or flaws. Avoid saying "Everything was great except…", and leave the negative thoughts unsaid. If you expect someone to do something for you exactly as you would have done it, you will almost always be disappointed. Accept that there are different ways to do things and learn to laugh about it. Focus on the positive to strengthen the relationship.

In all relationships, there will always be things that you will perceive as negative about the other person. If you choose to focus on them, then you are not choosing to have a relationship, nor are you choosing to appreciate your partner. We all have faults, and no one person can change another. Choose instead to focus on their positive attributes, and if necessary, make changes in yourself to accommodate where you perceive the lack in your partner. Expecting anyone else to behave in a specific manner that you desire is not accepting the other person's individuality. The greatest gift you can give each other is acceptance. When acceptance enters the relationship, those involved are willing to expand and do more, which is where positive change will evolve. When you know you are appreciated, your confidence builds and so does trust. It opens the door to communication and a deeper relationship that brings you closer together. Knowing that you can express yourself, without harming anyone else in the process and without fear of ridicule sets the foundation for a strong relationship.

Love and Sex

It is important to note that the words love and sex have not been mentioned up to now on the topic of relationships. The word *love* has often been used and misused in defining a relationship. A person can love a great number of people over a lifetime and at varying degrees. Understand that in a relationship you are two separate individuals with your own view of the relationship. This means that you will not always be in harmony. At any given time, one person may want to move at a faster pace while the other needs time to adjust. One may fall deeply in love before the other. One may be ready to transition to a deeper level of the relationship before the other. These are the constant ebbs and flows of a relationship. Patience, respect and consideration are the keys to communication. Happiness in a relationship is about having someone in your life who enhances your life, bringing laughter and joy, *and for whom you need to do the same for them each and every day.* Consider if you bring a smile to their face every day. Always take the time to be aware and consider your partner's needs and your actions toward him or her.

For centuries, people have had sex without love and have erroneously defined passionate sex and/or infatuation as love, yet have not obtained or been able to sustain a quality relationship. Sex is not representative of love. Sex can either be solely for the human action of physical satisfaction, without an emotional connection, or sex can be an enhancement of a relationship. Sex can add fun, passion and a deeper sharing of emotions between two people. If you think you are in love and you are considering sex with your partner, be certain to consider your decision carefully. Ask yourself how long you expect the relationship to last and be sure to ask the same to your partner.

You may be surprised at the answer. Emotions are powerful and the risks are high. If you are looking for a relationship, but all the components are not there for a solid foundation, make a decision that is rational and right for you.

When you peel back the word love and look underneath it for a definition, take a look at the feelings that cause the word to come forth. When you want to determine if you really love someone, consider whether or not you think of their wants, needs, desires and goals first, before you consider your own. When someone becomes so important, you care enough to learn what makes them tick and why. You then put their concerns right next to yours. You consider their feelings in making your choices *before you act and react*. It is only when you can achieve a relationship status where good character, appreciation, consideration, respect and trust exist that real lasting love can grow. You can re-engineer your relationship by slowly applying these principles whenever you are interacting with your partner. Be patient. Relationships take time and the application of these principles will help you build a strong partnership, which will enhance other areas of your life.

Education on Many Levels

One thing that is critical in your personal development on your way to achieving your dreams is to always remember that to go into anything blindly is to set yourself up for failure. Education, on the other hand, will serve you well.

You have had some type of parental influence that contributed to your education, whether it's from parents, older siblings, relatives, or perhaps a form of foster care. And you have all had some sort of education obtained outside of the home, from public or private schools, to college, to business training, or help from a mentor or the school of hard knocks. Education, from wherever it is obtained, is critical to the continual development of your thoughts and your ability to apply those thoughts to achieve a desired action. So when you consider your education for your overall character development and life path, there are many choices which will vary depending upon your age. Whether your choice is a public or private school, college, or the military service, which can provide a powerful education while providing the building blocks for integrity and decision making, you must be in charge of your education and responsible for your own destiny. You need to be aware of your options and do your own investigation to make informed choices that will best serve the vision you want in your life. *Do not expect anyone else to do this for you. Regardless of your age, it is not anyone else's responsibility. It is yours!*

The real world of education is happening around you every single day, every minute. You learn through events in your towns, villages and from countries all around the world. Through television, books, newspapers and the Internet, you obtain knowledge. Education can be gained by inviting people of all backgrounds and beliefs into your life, where you can obtain an insightful mix of views, broadening your knowledge base and increasing the depth of your life experiences.

Education never stops. All of your experiences have influenced and educated you to some degree. It is time to ask yourself: *Are you applying this education in a conscious manner when it comes to the choices you make, of the actions you take, and the words you speak, as to how they relate to that which you want to do?*

The automatic response is *Yes, of course I do,* but more often that not, in reality the answer is no. Each segment of your day may become isolated, where you are focused on only the task at hand. You may find yourself on autopilot at any given moment in your day, providing automatic responses to any given situation. If you are doing so, you are losing out. *Living in the moment and incorporating the focus of that which you want to do in any routine task opens you up to see opportunities to apply and even gain new knowledge that otherwise would have gone unnoticed.* This is a key to re-engineering your life. Never stop learning! Listen, question and gather as much information as you can at every opportunity. The more you learn about what you are interested in doing, the closer you will be to actually doing it!

Your experiences influence your views and form your judgements. Without an education and an open mind, those experiences can create and solidify prejudices, which can narrow your ability to see and seize opportunities. Education or lack thereof shapes character. Education has the power to remove insensitivity, racism, teasing, jokes, stereotyping, inconsiderate behavior, lack of action, silence, lying, omission, violence, controlling behavior, tantrums and aggression, all of which are born of ignorance. These are the things that hold us back, as a society and as individuals. The reality is you are human, and therefore, it is highly unlikely that these ever will disappear from your life. Be open to other viewpoints and options. Be willing to modify your own views, as your experiences broaden your knowledge base and allow you to create new judgements and new opportunities. Your integrity and strong character are important to your success. This part of your development of obtaining a continuing education can help enhance your special skill, talent or interest to re-engineer your life toward the success you seek.

Make a difference in your choices. You can design your life's direction by being aware and making educated choices. Since all actions have a reaction, *you can learn to create the reaction you desire.* Knowledge is key. Take a close look at the educational influences in your life.

Reflect upon the influences that have shaped you personally:

- How have those influences contributed to that which you are interested in?

- If so, how can they continue to further your goals now?

- How have those influences stopped you from doing what you are interested in?

- If so, how can you change your view of those influences or modify your goals to move forward?

To make the choices that best support your goals, you need to know as much as possible about all related subjects:

- Where are you now in your personal education as it relates to your overall goals?

- What short and long-term plans do you have to learn as much about the subjects that would support and further your goals?

- What are your options?

- Who can assist you?

You cannot make informed choices without knowledge. And without education, you will not be in control of your destiny. Education provides you with the ability to apply knowledge to any given situation. It gives you options! History is full of successful people without a formal education, *yet an education is a powerful tool to aid you in achieving what you want.* Never, ever let an opportunity for education, no matter what type, pass you by.

The Importance of Community

Webster's defines *community* as "a body of people living in the same place, a sharing in common."

You are part of a community by virtue of your existence. Communities may include countries, states, cities, towns, villages, schools, religious groups, political groups and any other group sharing a common interest. Almost every aspect where more than one person exists can be a community. Your use of facilities, stores, roads and consumption of goods is participation in a community.

Communities have been vital to the existence of human beings, as they allow a sharing of ideas and services. It is a give-and-receive relationship. Each community has a culture, a collective viewpoint that seeks to exert its influence for a gain of some type, while providing a service of some sort.

Those with a history of community participation have learned the advantages of belonging to community groups over time. They have seen the support a community can provide, and receive the satisfaction of knowing their participation has made a difference. This can be seen in older generations that have lived through difficult times. They will often have a stronger sense of the satisfaction that comes from community participation. Having been raised in a time where survival depended upon working together, helping each other out, these are the people who will still consistently donate to charities, volunteer their time, give blood and vote in every election. Younger generations raised in the Information Age have a different sense of community. While they may participate in community sporting events, the majority of their community time is spent online in a cyber community. While this has the advantages of reaching across borders of all kinds, including social, economical, political and even internationally across countries, it has the disadvantage of not knowing your neighbor.

Typically, you do not have a choice as to what country or area you live in, and therefore you are a part of those communities simply by your existence. Yet, it is the communities that you choose to actively participate in that you may want to spend some time focusing on, to see how they enhance or offer resistance to that which you are interested in doing. Some may be an important aspect of your overall character, such as a religious organization, while still others may serve no purpose for you or you for them.

Community Organizations

You may have joined one or several types of community organizations in the past. Periodically, it is important to re-evaluate which are assets to your overall vision and which may be a liability. If you are too busy to stop and think, finding yourself in a constant state of running like a mouse on a giant treadmill, unable to accomplish anything, or if you are being pressured into actions or decisions about your life, you may want to consider re-engineering this part of your life. By decreasing your level of participation, you can focus on what is really important to you. Take some time to list out the communities in which you actively participate. Put some thought into where you spend time. List out which organizations, clubs or group meetings are a part of your life. By putting them down on paper, you may be surprised at the actual number.

While you are making the list and reviewing the questions, it is important to take note on how you feel about them. Do you feel happy, excited, intellectually stimulated, obliged to participate, stressed, or otherwise not pleased? Your feelings are indicators of whether or not you may want to choose to continue your participation. Also ask yourself the following questions:

- Why do you participate in them?
- What type of influence do they have on you?
- Why are they important in relation to your overall satisfaction?

- Is your participation in them required or optional?

- How do you benefit from them?

- What are your contributions to them (aside from any monetary offerings)?

- Are they time eaters?

- Are they related to or support your interests in some manner?

- Can you work around any issues that may arise by no longer participating in them?

Religious, spiritual and other groups that may require you to modify your actions are often the most difficult to consider. Typically, your religious or spiritual influence begins with your family unit, whatever form you may have experienced. And typically, you would look up to that influence, accepting it without question. They provide a strong sense of community that may be the foundation for any beliefs you may have, but sometimes these groups and others will try to control your life rather than enhance it. Whatever groups you participate in, be aware of any hidden agendas or manipulations. By continuing to focus on your priority item from your *Interests* list, and being aware of where you are spending time and who or what has an influence over you, you can make conscious decisions and take appropriate action.

Expanding Your View

Your view of your community is based on your experiences with it. In order to see opportunities, it is important to expand your viewpoint. A simple way to start is by investigating what resources your community offers. Check to see what information is available to you through local organizations, clubs, business affiliations and government services. You may also find that you have personal resources. These would be people that you associate with, that can provide business services to you at discounted rates. Consider participating in events or meetings that will expand your professional contacts and social network. Providing a professional or volunteer service to the community, even at the simplest of levels, can be a catalyst to opening doors of opportunity. If applicable, start your own organization! The payback of setting your foot outside your door and interacting with others can be tremendous.

Beyond your immediate community there are an infinite number of experiences, contacts and perspectives. As much as you are able to do so, include travel on your agenda. Whether for business or pleasure, you can apply your heightened awareness and look for interesting opportunities wherever you are. The types of experiences that travel provides can greatly expand your views, as well as building a community network larger than the one you live in, from which you can draw from for contacts and support. Make it a point to be consciously and consistently aware of new or different perspectives, and consider how they can be incorporated into your priority item from your *Interests* list. By expanding your view and being selective about your community participation, you can expand your opportunities.

Your Social Network:
Is It Working For
or Against You?

When you look at the people with whom you surround yourself with, at home, at work and in all other aspects of your social life, think about if they contribute in some way to your personal growth. Consider if they fill you with happiness, excitement and energy, or if they drain you of your spirit, negating your dreams. The review of your social network is an important reflection in the process of re-engineering your life. It speaks volumes about you as a person. The individuals with whom you choose to surround yourself with are a direct reflection on you. An awareness of why you choose to surround yourself with them is also something you need to seriously consider.

Be clear and cautious in your evaluations. It's worth taking the time. Some things to consider are:

- Intellectually, how do you fit into the group?

- Are they people who challenge you, creating interesting dialogues, expanding your mind with new ideas and experiences?

- Do they support your interests, offer you balancing thoughts on your ideas, or provide opportunities for growth?

- Or are you the best in the group?

- If so, why?

If you have an ego that needs the supporting characters, you will never reach your dreams. Life is a constant training ground where you grow and learn every day. You are holding yourself back if you are the best in the group, as it is not a place where you will find opportunities to help further your interests. The people you associate with are a direct reflection of your character. If they are of negative quality, your character can also be in question by your association with them. If they have negative actions, your association can be viewed as condoning their behavior, and hence the quality of your character is diminished. Ask yourself if this what you want and if it is worth it.

Often at a younger age, people are influenced by what others are doing, thinking they need to do or have whatever is popular at that time in order to be accepted. This is also true of many adults in a consumer-oriented society. It can be as simple as the clothes they wear or the type of people with whom they associate, or even as dangerous as being influenced to experiment with drugs. Human beings have an innate desire to be loved and accepted, to the point that they will suppress their own individuality and even their dreams for it. That need for acceptance pushes us all, but especially young adults. It is often at this stage that the individual's thoughts and goals are set aside to participate in actions to gain acceptance. They wear their hair the same, dress in the same clothes, listen to the same music and participate in activities that have nothing to do with furthering their own personal goals. A couple examples of this are seen in the case of a young boy being dared to jump off a bridge to a shallow stream below, his friends taunting him. In another case, a young girl is being encouraged to snort a table product up her nose, because her friends are bored and they think it would be cool. In both of these cases, they have choices. The pressure is hard to deal with and the right words to escape the situation elude them. The old adage of *just say no* doesn't seem to suffice when they are faced with peer pressure. Often they cave in. Even then, they are convinced that the choices are theirs, never considering the social influences that are manipulating them. Had they learned how to deal with this and become engaged in an activity of their own interest and talents, they may have been able to say, "hey, I have better things to do with my time," and walk away.

Not only does this allow them to save face and be strong, it allows them to move beyond ridicule. By encouraging them to focus on their interests, their imagination, time and creativity can be spent on a project that could lead them down a better path.

Many adults have continued to make choices under this type of social pressure without truly being aware they are doing so. It becomes a habit to want to please others and conform to social pressure. And years down the line, looking back, many realize it was a waste of time. Where is the individuality, the uniqueness? Where are the trailblazers, those who are creating their own paths? When there is a fork in the road, too many appear to choose the frequently traveled path for immediate gratification, rather than one that may be more difficult, but would provide them with greater individual satisfaction in the long run. It can be a high price to pay to gain acceptance, setting aside their uniqueness and dreams, just for the attention of people *they probably won't even remember much less socialize with as the years move along!*

It takes courage and inner strength to re-engineer your life. Your social network is a major area to consider. A decision to move beyond a group that does not support your vision can be difficult. When you look at the people whom you associate with, and your thoughts are on your future, consider:

- What is the priority, your dreams or theirs?

- What are their values?

- What are their strengths?

- What does their sense of humor represent? (Is it funny or hurtful at the expense of others?)

- Are they controlling you or, are you controlling them?

- Do they contribute to expanding your interests?

Social Controls

If someone is manipulating you by any means (guilt, fear, money, love, or the need to be accepted), it is a negative. Manipulation can be done so subtly, you may not even recognize it. They may say, "If you loved me you would do this" or "You can't join unless you do … this or that." Pay attention to your feelings, they are a good indicator to determine if what you are experiencing is good for you or not. Remember to do things that *you* want and choose to do. If it is not your choice and the situation is not comfortable, find another solution. Also be aware of how you are influencing others. If you are the person influencing another, consider why you are doing it. Manipulating someone to control them may give you a sense of power, or perhaps you are doing it to gain attention. By being aware of this, you can choose to change your actions and words. In doing so, you may find that by taking a different approach can have a tremendous and positive affect on the atmosphere of a relationship. Both sides become more engaged in an equal footing when fear and guilt are removed from the process. It takes a concentrated effort in your choice of words and actions.

In your social interactions, be aware of your thoughts and goals when you consider the social groups with whom you are interacting. More than likely, the social environment you have is probably something you have chosen, because it is comfortable to you. Comfort provides you with a sense of security, a basic human need. Your social group can also be very stale and boring, preventing you from making changes to move toward your desires.

The Power of Choice

Your choices do make a difference. Consider that in many regards, humanity remains in an infancy state due to choices that are made by each and every individual. Globally, inequality in gender and race still exist, and poverty, disease and hunger still rage. Across the planet, people are following the various religious teachings of their leaders, all respectfully believing in what is taught to them by *their* elders. And unfortunately wars, which are rooted in these differences, still rage on. Freedoms are sacrificed for the illusion of safety and protection. Beliefs are the target of media manipulation, which bias us and removed us from each other. Through the centuries, humanity has been presented with opportunities to resolve these issues peacefully. Even now society has the opportunity for dialogue to help build bridges in these diametrically opposing views, *yet people have refused change because they do not want to give up the security in the comfort of what they currently know for the chance of something better, because it involves change.* They refuse change, rejecting choices simply out of habit, fearing change from their comfort zone, an insulated social network they have acquired and to whatever degree they feel accepted in. By not exploring new options and ideas, the problems remain. So in reviewing your social network choices, you may think that you are just one person making one small choice, but your choices have an effect on more than just you. The results of those choices are present in our every day lives, both personally and as a society. Take a look around. Your personal choices have an impact on your social network, which includes all of the communities in which you participate. Be aware that your choices affect and can influence your family, your community, your country and amazingly, even the world. Each individual can have a global impact.

Social networks are an important link in obtaining that upon which you choose to focus. When making your social choices, be open-minded and broaden your education in order to make wise choices based in facts, not emotions. Retain your individuality in your character development while ensuring that you honor and respect others, even if their choices are not your own. Be patient and tolerant of others. Be aware of your personal weaknesses, and be cautious of any manipulation from those that you associate with.

Re-Engineering Your Social Network

In order to work out of your comfort zone to make headway on your life path, some people chose a life coach, a person with whom you can work with to assist in focusing on that which you are interested in doing. You can also seek out mentors to help you focus on your interests, bounce ideas off of and learn from their experiences. There is tremendous value in this approach. Most often, people are eager to share their experiences and knowledge, presenting you with new ideas.

Take some time to list out the top ten current major people that you interact with now on a daily basis, and identify the influences they have on you and the contributions they make in your life. Include the areas you need to consider expanding on with them, and the work you need to do in strengthening the relationship without controlling it. Then take some time to consider the following when thinking about achieving that which you want to do:

- Whom would you like to associate with that you currently do not?

- Who can connect you to people with whom you would like to associate?

- What groups would be advantageous for you to join?

- Think of three people whom you may want to consider as a mentor.

- List five people you would like to meet to further the first item on your *Interests* list.

Make the effort to incorporate these people and groups into your life. Set up a meeting, even if it is only for a few minutes. Ask. Do not be afraid; just keep asking. Many people will be flattered that you did ask. Think and feel that your desire to move forward is stronger than your fear. Know that no one else is that concerned with you, they are worried about themselves. Let your fear and vanity take a back seat and step out to embrace life. Offer to volunteer your time. Help them out in return for their guidance. Host an event or invite them to an event that will further your interest. Be proactive and enthusiastic. When you are passionate and positive about something, people pay attention. Your interest, your vibration and your excitement are an energy others will want to be around.

Daily Actions and Choices

Have you ever noticed how there seem to be so many people who appear to have made one stupid mistake that has ruined their life? Take for instance the headline news reports in 2007 of a female astronaut, who in an obsessed, jealous state drove across state lines to confront a rival. Here is a woman who was intelligent and clearly up to the challenge of becoming an astronaut for NASA, but still fell victim to making an unwise decision. That decision to drive across state lines in an apparent attempt to confront and possibly do harm to her rival was, as most would agree, not the best choice she could have made. The consequences of such rash behavior driven by strong emotions were devastating. Her public humiliation combined with the loss of her job and legal charges of attempted murder, never mind the loss of a relationship, are all sad outcomes of a poor choice.

You see these types of situations night after night on the news. They appear to be the *one stupid mistake* a person has made which has seemingly ruined their life. What is even more interesting is that upon closer review, each situation was not the result of one stupid mistake. They were a culmination of poor choices made over and over again by each individual. And more than likely, they were not *aware* of them, meaning that they did not consciously consider all aspects and take into consideration their emotional state, which may have been aggravated by many other issues, nor did they consider all the possible consequences. Instead, a decision was made in anger or jealousy, followed by an action they will regret the remainder of their lives. Poor choices are born out of negative emotions. The power of negative emotions is strong. Those who continually make poor choices are allowing the habit of cultivating such negative emotions as anger, fear, jealousy and worry to *run* their life, which in turn eventually *ruins* their life.

Could the astronaut have made a better choice? Perhaps she could have been aware of all the signs of a bad relationship, valued herself more and could have decided to walk away from the relationship to work on getting into a better, healthier, and stronger one. Instead, her career is now destroyed, as well as having to face legal problems.

Understanding the Root and Results of Your Daily Actions

It is easy to sit back in judgment of others. It is much harder when it is your own emotions, your own situations, and your own passions. Know that *how you feel* is an indicator of whether or not you are in control of your thoughts. When you are experiencing strong emotions, feeling hurt, anger or jealousy, you are being controlled by your thoughts. Know that those thoughts are rooted in fear or insecurity. Acknowledge where it is coming from and know that right then and there, you still have choices and you can choose to focus on better feeling thoughts. Choose to be in control.

Every single person you encounter in your day is dealing with his or her own personal challenge. When you see someone acting in poor judgement, don't rush to judge them based on your perspective of the situation. Consider the driver passing by you at an unsafe speed, narrowly missing your car as they pass by. Yes, he or she could be an inconsiderate, irrational idiot and your temper rises. Road rage is a serious situation. Yet you really don't know their side of that situation. While you can be angry at their action and want to express your anger, don't rush to judge them so quickly. What if they have a life and death emergency, a need to rush to the hospital or help a child? You may never know, but you can be thankful they did not cause you any harm and wish them safely on their way… and hope the police are around the corner! Be the bigger person and let it go, along with your anger.

Other more subtle emotions can affect your life in ways you may not have considered. Arrogance and ego can come in to play and be equally destructive. Consider the simple act of a construction worker throwing garbage out of the window of his truck on the highway with the statement of, "It's not my town, who cares?" The construction worker does not see how his choice can ruin his reputation by not only losing the respect of his co-workers who were in the truck with him, but how it translates to his company, since the action was viewed by others on the road, much less the effect it has on the ecology.

Your choices determine your actions, which determine your character. Why should you care? Your actions draw results to you. Your choice not to take action also draws results to you. Right or wrong, judgments are made constantly of you by others, based on your actions and words, even your body language or the tone of your voice. People will make a judgment on your character and *may decide not to have anything further to do with you.* They may not tell you. You just might notice you're not invited to be around them anymore. You lose out on potential opportunities that you may otherwise have had. Be aware of how you present yourself to others at all times to determine if you are making the correct impression for the thoughts you wish to convey.

The daily actions you take and statements you make set your character in the eyes of others. Good, strong character is developed over time, based on your actions and decisions in what you say and what you do. Respect is earned and bonds to others are strengthened. *If you are not aware of this, then you are not aware that you are closing yourself off to opportunities, narrowing your choices to achieve that upon which you would really like to focus.* You are the one responsible for the doors closing in your face.

When you participate in a group, you are still responsible for your actions. Some actions that take place in groups often attain a lemming mentality. The lemming is a small rodent that runs in packs, following the leader to the extent they will run off a cliff to their deaths. Human groups that run in packs attain a mob mentality not so far from the lemmings. They attain a sense of anonymity, as if they are not responsible for their actions, since everyone else is doing it. This has been seen this in riots in the destruction of property, but it also appears quite simply with the driver of a car exceeding the speed limit. This type of driver will say they are doing so "because everyone else is doing it."

Be In Control

All actions have a motivation behind them. Before you take the action, consider what is behind it. Do bitterness and revenge influence it? Are you influenced by what the media is encouraging you to do? Walk away if it serves no purpose to achieving that upon which you choose to focus. You are more important. Do not let those thoughts and feelings manipulate you. Get over it and move on to what is truly important. In the process of working toward your vision, do so without harming or hurting anyone else.

You are in control of your destiny. What many do not realize is *that the daily actions and choices you make are the catalysts that define your direction.* You need to be able to control your thoughts. If you chose not to be in control, then you allow others to control you. You need to be able to consider options and the consequences of your actions. Understand that you have the ability and it is your choice how you use it.

One of the more interesting lessons in controlling your thoughts can be understood in the following example: John had completed all the course work and passed his open water test to be a certified scuba diver. He vacationed on a tropical island and went on his first dive under water. At eighty feet under water, he became absorbed in the activity, the colors and the creatures of the coral reefs. Then, for a moment he paused and looked up. The view is a bit distorted and the dive boat is just a speck above him. Quickly, he realized how far under the water he was and then all of a sudden, the water seems to push down on him, feeling like a heavy, suffocating weight. His heart rate accelerated and he begin breathing quickly, a knot of fear tightening in his stomach. *It was at this very moment that John had a choice!* He could continue the line of thought, spiraling down into a full-fledged panic attack, putting not only his life at risk, but that of his dive partner as well. Or he could make another choice. He could choose to take control of his thoughts. The word *focus* popped into his mind, followed by his favorite focus thought, bringing a positive feeling. It was enough for his mind to comprehend that *he could choose his thoughts and choose to control them.* That knowledge made him feel more confident and stronger as he forced his eyes away from the surface and back to the beauty around him, while taking a deep slow breath in and out as he was trained. He continued to concentrate on controlling his breathing, very slowly, very calmly while he let his eyes wander over the coral reef. His attention became absorbed in the activity and beauty of the reef, and his experience was that of pure enjoyment, the panic forgotten.

John's experience of recognizing and taking control over his fearful thoughts and emotions was a powerful experience. Awareness of your circumstances, the knowledge that you have choices in controlling your thoughts on the positive instead of the negative, and the satisfaction of implementing those thoughts to a positive outcome, is a tremendous experience. It becomes a *wow* moment of pride, showing you the path to a more joy filled life. These types of actions can take place all day long, with the multiple choices you are faced with daily.

The ability to snap out of it, to take control of your thoughts is a key tool in re-engineering your life and controlling your destiny. Remember these techniques:

- Recognize if your thought process is undesirable (be aware);

- Use your key trigger words, such as *focus!* or *stop it!* to redirect your thoughts;

- Take a slow, deep breath and calm your body;

- Use the same initial good positive thought to begin the change to a better thought;

- Continue to build on that with more positive thinking that you choose.

By doing this, you are controlling your actions. Your daily actions take you step by step either closer or farther away from whatever it is you want to do. The choices you make and the action you take will either lead you there or keep you away from it. It begins with awareness. Use your emotions as a guide. Anger, bitterness and revenge will not get you there. Positive thought will.

A Perspective on Work

The twentieth century began with mostly entre-preneurs, people providing goods or services to others and not much, if anything, in the way of social services. This is true of ancient history as well. If you had lived back then, you were likely to be a baker, a farmer, or some type of tradesman. Then the Industrial Age arrived, bringing facto-ries that provided new opportunities, options and choices for people. It was the transition from being self-employed to being the employee. It offered consistency, stability and opportunities that were previously unavailable to most people. The Information Age arrived, further solidifying the trend. Trade was on the rise globally and banking structures changed, both invigorating world markets with new concepts. Populations grew in record numbers. In the twenty-first century, the majority of people thought of whom they are going to work *for,* developing career paths. Then signs of stress appeared. The build up of false economic structures including inflated real estate prices, salaries, banking liquidity and consumer credit issues put the brakes on this economic conveyor belt. Suddenly lives were changed around the globe. As the world economies struggle to restructure, people are faced with having to reconsider what is important. It is a major awakening in many people's lives.

As a human being in this world, most of us need to provide some sort of service in order to receive compensation, which in turn provides us with the means to cover basic living needs. At this turn of events, many are finding there is no longer a demand for the service they have been providing. Others are hanging onto their jobs, but fearful of losing them.

Looking Forward

Work itself is all about time and compensation. You spend the time doing something for someone and receive compensation in return. If you are currently working, time can become the issue, working long hours that consume your life. You may feel the need to do this in order to receive the compensation you seek for the obligations you have. An ultimate goal would be to receive compensation for doing something you love. While it is not wise to walk away from any current compensation you are receiving, in your evaluation, you should be able to carve out time for yourself until you can make a move that will best suit you. If you are working, carve out the time in your workweek. If you are not, then you have time to invest in yourself, to create income from what it is that you are interested in doing.

Right away people think, *I don't have the time* or *I don't have the money*. What to do?

The first thing to understand is that you are *not* your job. In today's culture, too many people have defined themselves by what their job is, and when that job is gone or the career ended, they are stunned and do not know what to do. Understand that the job is only one aspect of your life. You are like a jewel with many facets and colors. There is much more to you than what you have done for work. Take a look at *Interests* list; you have interests and talents that reach far beyond any job.

Finding your way along the path to achieve that which you want can be frustrating. What you need to remember is that spark you felt deep inside that said, *Hey, wouldn't it be great if I could really do something like this?* Use that thought to keep you motivated in all aspects of your day and let the ideas flow. If you want to re-engineer your life, then change your attitude to a positive *can-do* focus, and be aware of the choices you are making. Re-evaluate your schedule and find the time to spend upon what you want to focus. Use the spark, that motivational thought to keep you on track. When you reach for the remote for your TV, think about how you could be spending the time toward what it is you really want to be focused on and make your choice in awareness. Where have you put yourself on your priority list? Things will not change unless you make the effort and focus on changing them.

Your focus needs to be worked into your daily routine. For starters, whatever you spend your time doing every day, even at work, be positive and excited about it. Do it well, and look at everyone as a potential connection. The attitude you convey in your behavior at work is noted by others and has a major influence not only on your mood, but also on those around you and can be a catalyst for something better. Have you ever been around someone who is excited by something? There is an energy, an uplifting feeling that is shared. The story of Harry and his routine cubicle life exemplifies this. Harry didn't care much for his job, but it paid well. He always arrived on time, did a good job, but kept to himself. He was always nice enough to deal with, but was not getting anywhere. His face was neither happy nor sad, he was just there. One day, he decided to start making changes. He hated change, but knew he wanted something better. He began by saying hello to people in the hallways in a cheery, upbeat manner as he walked past them. Most responded in kind, making him feel good. But one man never even acknowledged him. Harry kept on with his greetings. About two weeks later, the man actually said hello to Harry first. It was a small win, but it made Harry feel good. Harry set his next goal to expand the conversations. Over a period of time in these conversations, Harry learned more about his co-workers and they also learned about him. The positive energy he conveyed and his focus of doing something better lead to many opportunities. He eventually partnered with one of his co-workers to start a new business. None of it would have happened if he had not set out to change his mind set and his behavior to reach out in a positive way to engage his life with others. So, if you begin your day dreading your commute, change your focus to something positive about it. Use the time to think about options and opportunities to achieve that which you want to do. As you look around, you will find unlimited opportunities as long as you are positive and focused. It may be as simple as asking a co-worker for advice, or talking with someone during your day that can share information that benefits you, or making time to take classes at night.

You may also want to consider the age-old method of bartering. An example of this is a woman named Sarah. Her car broke down and as she was unemployed. She had no means to pay for the repairs, but she needed her car in order to look for work. When she heard how much it was going to cost to fix it, she wanted to burst into tears. Instead, she took a deep breath and considered her options. She talked with the owner of the neighborhood shop, who's family she had known for years. In doing so, she found that he needed someone to watch over his elderly parents, taking them to doctor appointments and such. They agreed on a barter of having the car fixed for assisting his parents for two-week time frame.

Options and opportunities are out there! Start simple and keep at it. Find one small thing to do each day and build upon it. Take whatever opportunity your current situation offers and look beyond the normal barriers. Often the problems you are faced with on the job are opportunities to create solutions. From them you may find a nugget of an idea that could become a business itself. With the changing times, the Information Age is a tremendous asset. Computers open up endless possibilities with global markets. Begin with the list of the things you want to do and look to combine them with your skills to seek out new profitable ventures. Combine efforts with others if need be. Approach it with the attitude of *Things can change; let's brainstorm some ideas.* Uncover all resources. Remove "I can't" from your vocabulary. If an idea doesn't work, modify it. Modify it as many times as you need to until it *does* work.

Many people are held back from going after their dreams by fear that can spring from a variety of different sources. Fear of failure, fear of success, shyness and fear of dealing with other people. Tackle this; don't let it hold you back. Acknowledge you have the fear and plan around it. Think first and foremost, what would you do if you *knew you could really do it?* Know that you can with persistence, awareness and effort. Know that you can achieve it. Any time you have nagging doubts, focus on what it is that you are interested in doing, and spend time thinking on it, expanding it. Let the excitement and energy of the thoughts give you the strength to focus even more, until step by step, you achieve what you want. This is how you make the effort. Hold the thoughts as often as possible. Make your choices in awareness. Turn off the TV and get engaged in your life!

If it is something you truly want to do, the excitement of your thoughts will give you even more energy to focus. Make the *effort* to *effect* the changes in your life, which will *affect* your life in the manner in which you choose.

The Health Factor

Human beings are an amazing and complex system of physical, mental, and spiritual components. Your physical body is incredible in its design. Your thoughts and emotions are factors that can affect how it operates. Likewise, your health plays a major role in your overall state of mind and in your ability to do things.

Your mind can have either positive or negative effects on your health. Bringing awareness about the connection between your thoughts and your health is vitally important, but few are aware of some common pitfalls.

In today's world, you are familiar with stress. It plays a major role in your life. You may stress about time, finances, family and numerous other things that constantly wear on you and affect your health. From a clenched jaw from tension to a suppressed immune system, along with an overtaxed cardiac system and lack of exercise, the effects are wide ranging. The stress you have is usually caused by the results of choices you have made. And usually, you have many options to change the stress factors in your life, but often don't. You do nothing to change your routine and become apathetic or spend time complaining to others rather than taking action to change it. Take the first step by raising your awareness using your feelings as a guide to begin to identify your personal stress factors. Take note when feelings of irritation or aggravation arise, and consider other options and choices you could make to reduce your stress level.

There are other factors affecting you from a physical standpoint that impact your health. By raising your awareness to identify these factors, you can recognize and make choices as to your actions. For example, one of those factors is naturally occurring, the highs and lows of hormones. Testosterone occurs not only in men, but women as well. High levels can induce unwarranted anger and aggression, especially when the levels spike. When aggressive feelings come over you, take the time to consider what is occurring internally, as well as external influences and *know that you have choices in your actions.*

Nutritional Aspect and Mental Focus

Another physical factor that you have control over is your source of nutrition. What foods you ingest play a large role not only in your physical well-being, but your mental state as well. Foods can slow you down, making you lethargic and disinterested in life, especially when too much is consumed. Foods loaded with caffeine, whether they are in the form of coffee, sodas, power drinks, chocolate or teas, and even some vitamins are commonly used to temporarily boost energy. Many do not think they can live without it and have developed a strong mental dependency, convincing themselves of their need. Most start with the need to be socially acceptable, whether it is caffeine, alcohol, or a form of tobacco. It may become a habit or a justified need in your mind, to which you may disallow any other option. You know the detrimental effects of all these things, but choose to hide behind the mental veil, using whatever justifications are at hand. Any dependency, no matter what the source, *leaves you without control.* Once it becomes a habit, it is controlling you, reducing your choices, narrowing your destiny. Whatever your reason for use, nothing is worth giving up control. If you do, you are existing, not living. Being in control of your health means being aware of what factors are affecting you, physically and mentally. Of all your priorities, your health should always be near the top of your list.

It is amazing when you consider the volume of outside influences that challenge us daily. Surprisingly, you can be seduced in a seemingly innocuous manner. There is a constant influence of advertisements by predatory companies selling products to help you with this or that ailment of which you previously never heard, but all of a sudden you are convinced you have! You are also inundated by advertisements for quick, prepackaged meals or other unhealthy items. Even your conversations with friends or family that seem to solely revolve around health issues can in itself be unhealthy. Educating yourself about health issues is good. Take control of the issue, and research it to the best of your ability. Empathizing with others on their issues is supportive, but whether the health issue is yours or theirs, obsessively focusing on it is detrimental to you both. If it dominates the mental well-being, it will affect the physical well-being. Cease to obsessively focus on your physical issues or those of others. This does not mean you ignore it. It means you need to deal with whatever the issue is and move forward. Do not let any physical ailment dominate your mind or your daily conversations. Instead, focus on positive thought, focus on what you want (like a strong, healthy, energetic body), and your mind will respond. In doing so, you will see more options for improving your physical health.

For example, by focusing on a desire for a healthier body, you will begin to pay attention to what you are eating and drinking. You might then begin to pay attention to what you are ordering at the restaurant or what you are buying at the grocery store. You might begin to get interested in new recipes. This might lead to conversations with friends on exercise routines or raise your interest to learn about other wellness options. This list can go on with endless options and opportunities. By focusing on your desire for a healthier body, you will start to see opportunities to change and you can gradually re-engineer your thoughts and actions to achieve that goal.

Regardless of your physical challenges, your mental state is key. Controlling and focusing your mind in the direction of something you want to do, as difficult as it may be at times, and working toward that goal will help strengthen you. Physical and mental health challenges can be overwhelming. Yet, time and time again, those with disabilities have overcome tremendous obstacles. Your awareness and application of a positive mental state can improve any physical challenges you have. By creating a healthier mental environment, your body will respond. By living in the state of awareness, you have the ability to analyze what influences you are allowing to have an impact on both your mental and physical well-being.

Your body is with you throughout your entire

lifetime. Putting yourself on the priority list means taking better care of yourself physically as well as mentally. Getting out of bed earlier, eating healthier, exercising to have more energy, turning off the television and making time for yourself are all choices you have. Give yourself the benefit of choices by being aware of what you are doing and thinking as it relates to your health. You can improve your health. It begins with positive thoughts. Think about what you want, know you can have it, and believe you can do it to whatever extent you choose. When the "I can't" or "Just this once" statements come in your head, focus back on the positive of what you want. It takes effort. When the desire for the cookie or the cigarette comes up, focus back on what you want: a healthy body, and make a better choice. When the pain is overwhelming, do what you can to ease it and then focus on what you want, a healthy body. Picture in your mind what you want. As your mental focus changes to a persistently positive feeling, and your actions and conversation do the same, your quality of life improves, which can have an impact on your overall health. Be aware of the negative influences around you, and choose the positive.

Religion, Science and the Art of Forgiving

When it comes to your health, an awareness of your daily thought process is important as it has an impact on the biology of your body. An interesting perspective on this meets at the crossroads of religion and science. Religion has been around in one form or another for thousands of years, whereas modern science is relatively new in a timeline comparison. Religion and science have been viewed as holding opposing beliefs, yet recently, work done in some scientific circles appears to support some religious teachings in regards to how our bodies are affected by our thoughts. Much of this is new, but worth considering in the context of being aware of your thoughts affecting your health. So consider the possibility that your thoughts can have a physical impact. We know that exercise can infuse our bodies with feel-good endorphins. We know that fright can send adrenaline pumping through our veins. Your body is made up of mostly of water, which is a conductor of electricity. These electrical currents run through your body, triggering nerves to move muscle. Electricity is energy! Now as science advances, work on the quantum physics level in the brain show indications that thought creates electrical bursts. If this plays out, your thoughts create energy. While science may not yet be ready to lay this out on the table, it is an interesting and thought provoking perspective on your health and the possibility of selecting the types of energy you can choose to send through your body. The chemical impact of our thoughts, whether it is as extreme as adrenaline or something else that gets generated in our bodies, leads us to begin to understand the power of positive focus, which for some is akin to the religious teachings of prayer.

Your health is not just physical; it is a combination of body, mind, and spirit. In this vein of thought, consider religious teachings on forgiveness. These teaching speak of forgiving as an important part of our development, yet are often met with thoughts of *Yes, I know I should forgive, but* … and truly you find that you cannot. You may harbor anger, hurt and numerous other emotions that keep your thoughts in a dark place. It is easier to understand now that those negative emotions can have a physical impact on your health with the potential of creating *dis-ease* in your body, each and every time you think of what caused your distress.

Understand that forgiveness is not about what you say to someone; it's about what you say to yourself. An example of this is a woman named Lola. For years she maintained on-the-surface good relations with her stepdaughter who lived with her. She loved her stepdaughter, but was angry over the way her stepdaughter treated her possessions with disrespect, albeit unintentionally. Things became broken and ruined beyond repair. It was frustrating, but in an effort to maintain a loving environment, Lola didn't say much. She knew one day that her stepdaughter would move out and wanted to maintain a good relationship. Lola valued the relationship over the things, but that did not stop her from harboring negative feelings. She found herself complaining to friends, even to the point where discussions centered on whom could top whom on the worst stories. Months after her stepdaughter moved out, Lola found herself in one of these conversations. After practicing to be more aware of her thoughts, she realized the negativity of the thoughts and abruptly stopped speaking. It dawned on her she was spending time on a subject that was history, had no positive angle and felt like she was touting a victim badge. She didn't want to do that anymore. It was done, over. She loved her stepdaughter, and Lola found that she was the one now being disrespectful. She looked at the woman with whom she had been speaking and told her exactly that, then walked away. As Lola pondered her thoughts, she realized at that moment that she had forgiven her stepdaughter. She dropped her victim badge and baggage she had been touting for years, mentally feeling it fall off her shoulders and slamming to the ground with a thump. She felt the negativity leave her body. It was the first time she truly understood forgiveness. It wasn't about her stepdaughter. It was about her thoughts about her stepdaughter. She knew she wouldn't forget the past, but the anger inside was gone.

Forgiveness is about letting go of unhappy feelings by realizing what is important and appreciating any positive aspect. You start by feeling the anger and laying the blame. Depending upon the transgression, this could take a good deal of time, especially if it is of a more serious nature. Then one day you realize that it is old news, and by continuing to hold your anger you are not only giving it life again, but you are letting it control you present. Understand that the other party involved who inflicted the injustice probably never even thinks about it or cares. Healing begins when you recognize that you are the one holding onto the past transgression against you, and that the past is over and nowhere near as important as your present and your future. If you are focused on the past, you are not in control of your life. Holding on to a position of being a victim or waiting for someone to right what you perceive as a wrong they have done upon you is a waste of time and energy. You are holding yourself back and letting the past dominate your life. In everything around us, there is good and bad. Where you choose to focus is up to you. In relationships with people, whether they are friends, family, or associates, you can focus on the negative and harbor ill will, or you can choose to look past their faults and enjoy the goodness in them to enrich your life. Forgiveness is about releasing negative emotions and thoughts, accepting things you cannot change and moving forward with your life in a positive manner. Your physical health is dependent upon your mental and spiritual health, so be aware of your emotions, thoughts and feelings to keep your body in a place of good vibrations. Dump the victim badge. Not for them, but for yourself.

Your Health Factors

Re-engineering is about starting where you are at right now and gradually heightening your awareness to modify your thoughts, feelings, choices and actions to achieve what you want. When you consider the health factor in the process of re-engineering your life, look to the three main areas, physical, mental and spiritual, to determine if there are any that you can focus on to help you reach your overall objective from your *Interests* list.

If you are dealing with a physical issue, aside from working with your doctor, consider asking a friend or relative to become your personal advocate to assist you in research and aid you in dealing with the medical community. Expand your options and look to both Eastern and Western medicine. Also consider a nutritionist, preferably one that works with your doctor, for dietary changes and the use of supplements to help alleviate your symptoms.

Mental factors include stress and emotions. Stress comes from a variety of areas. Determine which contribute to the highest levels of stress. If they are factors that you can change, start working step by step to make those changes. If they are factors you consider out of your control, then think of ways to help relieve the stress, such as physical exercise or deep breathing exercises, meditation or mental breaks to shift your thoughts elsewhere. Seek a support group or a professional to help you work through any issues you are working on.

Emotions of depression, anxiety or fear can wield control over your actions. Hormone levels can cause mood swings and heighten or lower your mental clarity. On any of these issues you should work with your doctor and perhaps even a nutritionist to begin the steps toward that which you want to improve. Remember to employ the Spiral Up technique discussed in an earlier chapter to help toward controlling and focusing your thoughts.

The spiritual factor is like the propeller that pushes you along as you navigate through your life. Your spirit is the part of you that is driven by your emotions. The things you care about and your feelings have an affect on your biology. For this reason alone, it is good to seek out and spend time on those things, or with others that help inspire you to keep your spirit strong and distance yourself from those that do not. Maintaining a high level of inspiration will help drive your internal energy force and keep you on track to your interests.

Understand that the physical results of any changes you integrate in your life take time. Be patient and kind to yourself, taking one day at a time. More than likely you did not get into whatever issue you choose to work on overnight, so do not expect and overnight resolution. Be focused and take your re-engineering process step by step.

Investment in Self

In the first chapter, you were asked what you would like to be *doing* with your time. You identified your key interests, the things that make you tick. Now it's time to take a look where you are spending your leisure time, to determine if it is in keeping with your dreams and goals, or if are you easily sidetracked or influenced. Take a look at your average week, to see how you are spending your time. What is your routine? By looking at a snapshot of your life and viewing it from the perspective of awareness, you can ascertain if you are truly using your time in a manner that will achieve your desires, or if you are spending it waiting for something and wasting your time.

When you look back at the last week, how much of your time was actually spent on anything to do with any item on your *Interests* list?

If you are surprised at how little time you were able to spend on it, take a closer look at where you did actually spend your time. It is not only important to determine what you spent your time on, but also why and how it influenced you. It is a worthwhile exercise to list out all the non-business, personal activities you do each week.

For each day, list out how you filled your personal time and how much time it consumed. Take out a paper and write across the top of the page each day of the week, Sunday, Monday, Tuesday, etc. Fill in the activities for each day, noting the time you spent on it and why. You may also want to note how you felt about it. You may find that some of your activities actually took more time than you expected, or that you spend more time on it than you thought. As you review the list, consider the following:

- Are of them as necessary to your relaxation and happiness?

- Would any be helpful to achieving your interests?

- Were any a waste of time?

- Can you see where you could clear out an hour a day to focus on that which you want to do? If not, consult with someone you are comfortable with. Often another pair of eyes can help you identify areas of potential change.

- Are these activities something you have chosen or someone else has chosen for you?

Look over the list above, and for each item that you have entered for the week, ask yourself how you feel about it. Good, bad, or indifferent? Your feelings are a good indicator as to whether you may or may not want to continue participation.

Simple things can have an effect on how you invest in yourself. For example, let's say you spent some time listening to music. This could have been while driving in the car, at home, or at a concert hall. Consider what your choice was in doing so; if it was to relax or for the enjoyment of it while you were doing something else. Think about how you felt and what your actions were during and directly afterwards. Music influences your emotions. It has the power to raise your spirits and make you want to dance. It can make you calm and relaxed, even aid in meditation. It can also bring you down and depress you, or stir up angry and aggressive behavior. *So your choices in music can and will influence your choices and actions while you are listening to it, and even directly after you have listened to it.* It will affect your actions and even how you speak to others. Be aware of your music choice and its influence over you. It may be an expression of your mood, but it will influence your upcoming moments or day. *Change the music, which changes your attitude, which changes your behavior.* This is an example of a very simple way to re-engineer your life.

Another influence to look at is the media. Take a look at the movies, TV, books or other forms of media you use. These have a huge influence on you. Some media items are of less than quality content. There is no nurturing growth of self when one is exposed to negative behavior and violence. It's no secret that bad programming can influence behavior negatively. Consider why you are choosing your media selection:

- What do you get out of your media choices (passing time, entertainment, educational)?

- Are you vicariously living through someone else's actions in the movie, book, or video game (when you could be working toward doing it yourself)?

- Is your media choice mentally stimulating or does it solely provide entertainment?

- Is your media choice in any way connected to furthering your dream?

- Can you make a better media choice?

- If so, what would it be?

- Can you make better use of your time, selecting something else to do?

- If so, how?

Being conscientiously aware of how you spend your time and why you spend it that way is important. Taking time to contemplate recent events and consider changes in your direction and choices is critical to remain focused. Only you can control how you spend your time. You make the choices and you can modify your habits. Get away from the media. Get away from others who do not allow you to focus on what you are interested in doing. Move to a higher place, away from poor programming. You may find that instead of discussing the latest sitcom antics, you might end up in a discussion on *your* project, making contacts and discussing new and exciting ideas as you focus on re-engineering your life. In order to achieve your vision of what you want in life, choose activities that educate, inspire and entertain in a positive manner. Focus on moving forward, step by step, one day at a time. Invest wisely in yourself, be willing to change and grow. Be positive and enthusiastic as you make the time to work on what you are interested in. Do it with knowledge, confidence and certainty, because you know you can modify your goal as new ideas help you create an even better vision than when you started. Be patient with yourself. This is the joy of the journey, the process of creation. This is *living* your life.

Staying Motivated

The daily grind of obligations eats away at your time. You blow off devoting any time to whatever it is that is on your *Interests* list. One day goes by, no big deal. Then another day goes by, and another until the days, weeks, months and years pass, and you find yourself no closer to achieving what it is you want to do. The temptation is strong to bury yourself in TV, games or other activities. You think that there is not enough time or money to do what you really want. Then you wake up one day in the same old rat race with the feeling that life is passing you by. All your hopes and dreams have gone nowhere. You are existing, surviving, but not living in joy. This doesn't have to happen!

So what can you do?

Know that you will lapse; know that you will fall off course. That's okay. When you do so, recognize it and adjust. See it as a positive! Allow some downtime. Take the time to regroup your thoughts. Consider options and adjust priorities. Maybe scribble out some notes on your thoughts. Review accomplishments. Allowing yourself this time will eventually lead you back to the things you want to do, where you interests are.

True motivation *comes from within you,* not from anyone else. It is no one else's job or responsibility. It is up to you. It begins with the spark of thought you have that ignites your imagination when you consider what is on your *Interests* list. The excitement you feel with those thoughts and ideas, that energy is what will help propel you forward. Your feelings are a great indicator of what you need to do in order to keep motivated. Anytime negative thoughts or fears rise within, banish them by focusing on what you want to do. Be aware of your thoughts. Know you can control them and focus them on what you choose. This is the key. Replace them with the excitement of your vision. Feel the positive energy inside you and take steps to accomplish a part of the task you are interested in doing. Your confidence and excitement will grow with each step. Knowing that you can control your thoughts to keep the excitement and anticipation level up gives you the strength to be persistent. By being positively and persistently focused, you will keep yourself open to new thoughts and new opportunities that further strengthen your commitment to see it through and achieve that which you want to do.

One day you may find yourself sitting in front of the TV or doing something that is wasting your time. By having previously spent time focusing your thoughts on what you really want to do, your subconscious will be working, even while you spend some down time. As you sit in front of the TV, your mind may occasionally go back to the item on your *Interests* list. You may experience a guilty feeling because you are watching TV and not working on your interests. You mind will nag you to turn off the TV or nag you to put down the game and work on your priority item. You ignore it, over and over again with whatever excuse you can think of. Yet your desire to change this aspect of your life and achieve your goal will persist, and you will become your own Nagigator™ with thoughts that will propel you to take action. Then one day you may actually turn off the TV and spend time on what you really want to do! Thoughts will pop in your mind simply because your focus has been on your project. Keep it up and you will find your habits slowly changing, encouraged by small satisfactions from each step you accomplish.

Stick with it! Looking at it today, you might not know exactly how to achieve whatever it is you want to do. If you persevere and keep moving forward, step by step each process will unfold, allowing you to make choices and move forward, modifying your ideas as different opportunities become apparent. Others may try to discourage you, even give you a hard time. Keep your focus on thoughts that inspire you and keep moving forward. A favorite example of this was a woman named Sheryl. She wanted to join the police force. She could out-shoot and out-drive anyone in her class in the academy. She passed every test with high marks, except one.

She could not run very fast. But she would not give up. She ran as fast as she could. During those runs, she was subject to others yelling and screaming in her face that she was a failure and she should just quit. Her response was always, "Yes Sir!" but she kept on running. She refused to stop. She came in last every time on the runs, but she never quit. She graduated and became an excellent police officer.

It is up to you to stay focused and feel the excitement and anticipation of moving forward on that which you want to do. It can be helpful to seek out resources for ideas and support. Find a mentor, set up a schedule for yourself and search out opportunities and options to any obstacles. Be creative. Join groups that support your interests; learn as much as you can about whatever it is you are interested in doing. From the time you awake until the time your day is at end, you will find the motivation in the excitement and anticipation of your thoughts, as you consider the one thing you most want to do and the options you uncover. As you do so, know that the people who are successful at achieving what they want, focus and take action on it each and every day. Know that it is your effort in focusing your thoughts that will get *you* to succeed.

Bottom Line

The most important thing that you can take away from this book is being aware and understanding the influences that can control you. Only you are in control of your thoughts and those thoughts can affect the outcome of any given situation, which may or may not bring you closer to that which you are interested in doing. You have the control. You have the choices and you can live in the present, not the past. Being able to do the things you want will be the catalyst for obtaining the things you want to have.

So what will it take for you to do something, to take control of your life, and to re-engineer it in a manner that you desire? Perhaps it is fear of losing a job, or having lost one, coupled with a desire to have a more satisfying life that will be your catalyst to change. Only you can determine the factors that will eventually motivate you.

The reality is many people are not going to completely shake up their routine or lifestyle. They are basically satisfied with their lives even if they are not living in joy every day. Fear of change and comfortable circumstances seem to freeze them in limbo, and they busy themselves with the day-to-day routine of survival and obligations. Unfortunately, those not willing to put forth the effort will continue to experience the nagging *I could have* thoughts, causing feelings of heartache, not joy. As the years go by, it's the same old routine and same unfulfilled dreams. Even a loss of a job could cause them to spiral downward in negative thoughts and actions.

Like it or not, life has changed dramatically for most. The way business is done has changed, affecting jobs worldwide. Take heart though, because even with these changes there are new opportunities. You can adapt to these changes and succeed in your goals. You can do so by understanding the depth of awareness that you utilize in your day-to-day life, in your decisions and actions. Apply these insights toward that which you want to do and you will be able to see the opportunities that come with change.

Happiness doesn't come from success, nor does it come from money, your partner, your friends or your job. Real happiness comes from within you. Sometimes it is buried so deep, you have to drag it out. It takes focus. It takes practice. It takes awareness. Your beliefs about happiness, or any subject are a result of your thoughts. When your thoughts are focused long enough on any subject, it becomes a belief. By being aware of your thoughts and changing them to the direction you choose, you can ingrain new beliefs within you.

Each of us has the capacity to make changes to bring joy and anticipation into our lives daily. Each of us has the ability to do something in order to affect change. Real change occurs over time and it will only happen if you put the effort into it. The longer you think and apply changes to your life, the more successful you will be at achieving results. Every day is important. Every day you need to be aware of the influences affecting you. Every day, your ability to know why you are making your choices is another day of living in the moment, of living life, not just existing, but living in full awareness. Each day will come with its anticipation, rewards and satisfaction. Each day will build upon the last if you put forth the effort and focus, becoming clearer and stronger. Understand that *focus* is the key to reaching your full potential. *Stop existing and start focusing your thoughts in an upward, positive spiral!* By focusing your thoughts in a positive manner, your emotional feelings will strengthen! Have you ever noticed someone who just seemed to generate a positive electric energy? All eyes are drawn to them and everyone feels uplifted. You can generate this energy in yourself by focusing on that which you are interested in with inspiring positive thoughts. Those positive thoughts will literally make you feel like your body is electrified with an energy, a vibration. Others can sense this and are drawn to you, affording you with new opportunities. Your enthusiasm will generate more creative thought, possibly even keeping you awake at night with the excitement!

Energy is the driving force. You are the one who can control it. Electrified energy can fill a room with excitement, and you can feel the same energy within you. Author Wallace D. Wattles called it "that thinking stuff from which all matter is created." Your thoughts can energize you, and sharing your thoughts can also energize others. From those thoughts ideas are born, opportunities are noticed, the momentum grows and things can be created.

Some people who have items on their list consider them goals. *Goal* is a four-letter word, but then so is *path*. Don't let the goal get in the way of the path you choose and don't focus too much on the goal looming ahead, thinking it is out of reach or too big. You may not understand how to get there from where you are right now, but don't give up. In our immediate, "I want it now" world of gratification, it is important to continue moving toward what you choose to focus on. Find the thoughts that will encourage you to continue on your journey and the path will become clearer with each step of progress you make. The more positive thoughts you have to inspire you and the more they are brought to the front of your conscience, multiple times a day, the easier it is to change your focus, actions and even reactions to everything around you. The more you think, act and focus on what you want to do, the closer you are to achieving it. And the more interesting, exciting and fulfilling your life will be.

As you move forward, be flexible and take one step at a time. Do not worry about the complications you may face, just keep chipping away each day toward that which you are interested in doing. Make use of your time. Focus on what you are interested in doing and you will be more aware of the opportunities that will arise. One of the pure joys in life can be found in unexpected events. Events, whether they are perceived as good or bad, present opportunities to us. Sometimes the event may appear to be terrible, but it can bring forth an opportunity that you would otherwise not have been able to see. It is up to each of us to see and seize them. Be flexible and make informed choices. Use your downtime wisely as an investment in yourself with an eye toward the consequences. Find your number one priority from your *Interests* list and stick with it until you finish it. The finished version may not be the same as the original concept, because you would have continued to create and modify it during the process. That is the joy of creation, the excitement and satisfaction.

Be aware of the influences from your family, your relationships, your education, the community in which you live and the social network with whom you surround yourself. Notice how your thoughts and the choices you make in your daily actions can affect your health. Know that real change is a learning experience and regardless of your age, you should always continue to learn and grow, further enriching your life and investing in yourself. Change happens over time with you being aware of the influences and making choices. You are a creature of habit. Old habits that are established have been created early and are hard to change and can eat away at precious time. Remember that if you do nothing, you will be very limited in achieving anything. You don't have to do anything but exist. Yet as a human, you are creative and that creative spirit drives you to wanting more, to do more and to experience more. Recognize that habits are hard to change, but know that instead of spending time worrying, complaining, or doing nothing, you can choose to do something and step by step accomplish it. If you commit to change and follow through with your actions, doors of opportunity will open up. Be in control and replace the old habits with new ones that serve a better purpose for you.

As you move forward, consider the following:

- Create a vision board or a notebook to list all the things you want to have and do, along with pictures and any inspirational phrases, thoughts or affirmations that encourage you. Use it daily, reviewing and adding to it.

- Focus every morning on the item you chose as the priority from your *Interests* list. Consider any new angles or opportunities to investigate for the day ahead.

- Keep track of your progress on a calendar, noting where, with whom and how you are spending your time. Review weekly, making adjustments necessary to achieve more the next week.

- Investigate each week new opportunities, classes, meetings, social networks or any other angle that will aid you in achieving your goal.

- Remain positive and focus on the excitement you feel moving closer to your goal.

- Keep your energy level high, avoiding any pitfalls discussed earlier in this book. Re-read sections of this book as often as you need to keep an open mind and your focus strong.

Remember that anyone who has been successful at anything is successful because they have been focused. Being aware, having the knowledge to focus your thoughts and applying them in a positive direction is powerful. Don't get caught up in the greed of the goal or the possessions you want to have. Stop with the excuses. Be your own Nagigator™ and focus on the journey, taking one step at a time. Live each day in appreciation for all things, including the diversity around you. Focus on what you are interested in doing. Get the courage to go after what it is that you are interested in by concentrating on the inspirational spark you feel at the thought of doing something you enjoy.

You have the power to re-engineer your life.

You have the ability to see and seize opportunities.

Take control and enjoy the journey!

Recommended Reading

Re-engineering Your Life to See and Seize Opportunities has been written so that you can open the doorway in your mind to advance your knowledge and achieve your dreams. It is only a beginning. There are dozens of books that tackle how to go about doing what you want or focusing on what you want. Some of the good ones are listed here. There are others that delve into the power of thought. For those of you willing to excel and take the next step in re-engineering your life, read on!

Three Cups of Tea, One Man's Mission to Fight Terrorism and Build Nations… One School at a Time, by Greg Mortenson and David Oliver Relin, Penguin Group Inc., 2006. The tenacity of focus and the strength of character that are detailed in this man's journey of achieving a seemingly impossible desire reinforces the power of focus and the richness of personal satisfaction in achieving that which you want to do.

Ask And It Is Given: Learning to Manifest Your Desires, by Esther and Jerry Hicks (The Teachings of Abraham), Hay House, Inc., 2004. This book is part of an amazing series that details how very important each and every thought is. To fully understand how your thinking may be holding you back. This is a must read and very enlightening.

The Science of Getting Rich, Attracting Financial Success Through Creative Thought, by Wallace D. Wattles, Destiny Books, 2007. This book was written over one hundred years ago, yet this reprint is still relevant today, offering information on the power of focusing thought and selecting actions to obtain goals.

Jack Canfield's Key to Living the Law of Attraction, A Simple Guide to Creating the Life of Your Dreams, by Jack Canfield and D.D. Watkins, Health Communications, Inc. 2007. This is a step-by-step book that will help you move forward in the process of focusing thought and implementing actions in achieving your goals.

Banker to the Poor, Micro-Lending and the Battle Against World Poverty, by Muhammad Yunus with Alan Jolis, Public Affairs, 2007. Fascinating and compelling memoir of the birth of Grameen Bank, its history and the wide-reaching social and economic impact it has had and is still having today. Truly shows that we all have the ability, even in small actions, to make a big difference.

What the Bleep Do We Know!?, by William Arntz, Betsy Chasse and Mark Vicente, Health Communications, Inc., 2005. As humans, we will always be asking questions. This book will stretch your mind.

Change your Mind, Change Your Life, by Gerald
G. Jampolsky, M.D. and Diane V. Cirincione,
Bantam Books, 1993. This book explores the
concept of Attitudinal Healing, an extremely
insightful book on positive thinking.